DRINKING FROM
A DIFFERENT WELL

Simmons invites us to take a clear-eyed view and challenge the balance of competitive and collaborative narratives for the sake of our collective future. A must read for anyone who cares about using the power of story in a conscious and generative way.

—MARY ALICE ARTHUR, AUTHOR OF *365 ALIVE! FIND YOUR VOICE. CLAIM YOUR STORY. LIVE YOUR BRILLIANT LIFE.*

"Annette Simmons' new book, *Drinking from a Different Well*, is the must read book of the year. No need to read between the lines or wonder what the author is telling you – Simmons spells it out in story after story, told by women who embrace power to achieve moral goals. Simmons demonstrates that the stories we tell ourselves define us and either expand or limit the power we need. This book proves the stories women tell matter. Women's words matter. Women's ideas matter. #Smashing #Brilliant #Explosive"

—YVONNE DIVITA, WRITER, AUTHOR AND BOOK COACH AT NURTURING BIG IDEAS

"It's time to change 'business as usual.' Simmons brings women's studies into the business classroom. If you loved Carol Gilligan's *In a Different Voice*, you'll love Simmons' *Drinking from a Different Well.*"

—AMY WATERMAN, YOURBRILLIANCE.COM

"Annette Simmons offers a thought-provoking exploration of how power is expressed depending on what underlying beliefs, values, and attitudes shape the stories we tell about power. As a bonus, Annette offers astute and powerful insights through her vivid analysis of the many story examples. A valuable read for all genders!"

—KENDALL HAVEN, AUTHOR OF *STORY PROOF AND STORY SMART*

"Through compelling stories and careful analysis, Simmons gives voice to a practical and moral approach to power. This important book inspires me to appreciate my own power and to see and cultivate power in others."

—THALER PEKAR, PIONEER IN NARRATIVE AND COMMUNICATION

"*Drinking from a Different Well* is an in-depth guidebook to identifying, nurturing and honoring the type of people we can trust to implement decisions in the public interest. After fully consuming this book I am inspired to ask myself what next action will I choose if I am able to exorcise the motivators of greed and stupidity in myself?"

—APRIL LORENZEN, CHIEF DATA SCIENTIST AT ZETALYTICS

"Annette narrates the core issues that challenge women's interpretations of power. Many women choose to steer away from definitions of power that inflict pain to use their power to protect others and protect the planet. Annette maps a much bigger picture than the small maps of competitive narratives to reveal a way forward. How can we bridge the competitive and the collaborative? How do we value the power women treasure most? For sure this book is a real treasure."

—KRISTIN ENGVIG, FOUNDER GLOBAL WIN (WOMEN'S INTERNATIONAL NETWORKING) & WIN CONFERENCE

"The behaviors and mindsets—I'm tempted to call them male pathologies—that made workplaces hostile to women in the past are now clearly writ large on the national and world stage. Because of the domination of these games—competition, power-over, win/lose, zero sum, us vs. them, profit goals, my country first meaning my country only—we are face to face with threats to our liberty, our safety, our health, our well-being, and our very existence. We desperately need water from this other well—collaboration, emotion reasoning, power-with, moral goals—eloquently put forth in *Drinking From A Different Well.*

—MICHAEL GUSHUE, RETIRED USAID POLICY ANALYST AND POET

"Annette Simmons's new book *Drinking from a Different Well* demonstrates how storytelling inevitably reveals that the answers we seek are rarely found in either/or, zero sum games, but rather in 'an endless balance between the best attributes of two sides of a paradox.' Through the real stories of powerful women, this book illustrates that rather than replace the competitive reasoning of men, combining it with the collective narratives women tend to prioritize can chart a new path to solve the global problems we face."

—RAIN BENNETT, HOST OF THE STORYTELLING LAB PODCAST AND AUTHOR OF *SIX SECOND STORIES: MAXIMIZE YOUR IMPACT IN MINIMAL TIME WITH VIDEO STORYTELLING.*

"Annette Simmons combines her talent as a first-rate researcher with her talent as a masterful storyteller. She celebrates gender differences instead of judging them. And typical of Simmons' books, she doesn't stop at just giving us provoking thoughts to ponder but provides practical ways to apply these insights to address challenges ranging from day-to-day stressors to major global issues. If you want to position yourself to move forward with new, bold, perspectives that create real change, read this book.

—SYBLE SOLOMON, CEO, LIFEWISE STRATEGIES AND CREATOR OF MONEY HABITUDES

"In this time of extraordinary divisiveness, I, like so many, wonder, 'How did we get here? And how do we move forward in a healthier and unifying way?' Annette Simmons offers answers to both questions by looking through the lens of how men and women differ in our definitions and lived experiences of power and powerlessness. While some will rankle at her suggestion that classically male narratives of competition and zero-sum outcomes created many of the global problems we experience today, those who are open-minded will find a call to merge strengths found along the gender spectrum into strategies that are as necessarily-nuanced as the problems we face."

—SB RAWZ, BUSINESS & EMPOWERMENT COACH

Additional books by Annette Simmons

Territorial Games
Understanding and Ending Turf Wars at Work

A Safe Place for Dangerous Truths
Using Dialogue to Overcome Fear and Distrust

The Story Factor
Inspiration, Influence, and Persuasion Through the
Art of Storytelling

Whoever Tells the Best Story Wins
How to Use Your Own Stories to Communicate
With Power and Impact

DRINKING FROM A DIFFERENT WELL

How Women's Stories Change What Power Means in Action

ANNETTE SIMMONS

Published in the United States by Collaborative Narrative Solutions of Raleigh, NC.

Names: Simmons, Annette, author
Title: Drinking from a Different Well: How Women's Stories Change What
    Power Means in Action
Includes bibliographical references and index.

LCCN: 2021918376 (print)
ISBN: 978-1-7378157-0-9 (print) | ISBN: 978-1-7378157-1-6 (ebook)

Subjects: Power (Social Sciences) Leadership (Business)
Printed in the United States.

Differentwell.com

Book and cover design by Jeffrey Jenkins Projects.
Illustration by Channarong Pherngjanda.

For Greta Thunberg.
I hope this helps.

"Making my father proud."

CONTENTS

INTRODUCTION

Back in 2001, I gathered hundreds of stories that revealed women's experiences of "power-in-action." Many of these stories did not reflect what I had been taught to believe about power. The main difference was this: While traditional narratives portray power in the context of adversity and battles, women's true stories about power recruit narratives that define power as the ability to nurture and protect, as well as the ability to control or dominate.

I was offered a book contract and submitted my manuscript in 2003, only to hear my editor insist that I "tone it down." Clearly, writing about gender was dangerous twenty years ago. I was already losing business by questioning male biases, and I didn't want to rock more boats than I thought I could handle. So I bailed on the project and returned the advance.

Today I believe there's nothing more important than rocking the boats of those who believe that power is only about dominance and control. Beginning in 2017, with the help of my dear friend Laura Guyer, we did the research again, from scratch, with a whole new batch of women's stories. Laura's work at Training Resources Group expanded our access to an international pool of powerful women. We also added some men's stories for comparison. This second round of research followed the same methodology I'd used before. We asked our network of clients and friends to "name a powerful woman who might be willing to share a story." After we interviewed the women they nominated, we asked those powerful women to nominate other powerful women. This created a crowd-sourced sample of women who may or may not perceive themselves as powerful but who were perceived by their peers as being powerful. We asked each woman two questions: "On a scale of one to ten, how powerful are you?" and then "Can you tell me a story about a time you were powerful?" We interviewed women from seven different countries and of multiple ethnicities, with an age range from twenty-three to seventy-six. I also interviewed a smaller number of powerful men for comparison purposes.

Once again, I found that true stories about real life often reveal truths that run deeper than traditional theories and dictionary definitions. For many women (and men who value feminine perspectives), power means more than the ability to achieve material goals. For us, real power also comes with the ability to achieve moral goals. Once powerful groups become increasingly more dependent on automated decisions, we diminish the impact of moral reasoning that predicts and avoids excessive greed and selfishness. Decision-making and power structures must integrate intuition, moral conscience, and nurturing instincts— what my research shows are feminine values—or power systems will be guided by immoral reasoning. Already systems that aggregate and reinforce disinformation are justified as profitable and therefore as rational business models, even when the results threaten necessary levels of social trust.

I want to rescue this word "moral" from negative connotations of judgment and control back to the original source of morals: storytelling. My definition of a moral is a storied lesson passed down from our ancestors in order to help us imagine how our actions today will impact our tomorrows. Morals passed down in story form preserve the ambiguity (i.e., balance of polarities) necessary for making moral decisions. Our love affair with certainty has been destructive. Turning morals into rules reduces the wisdom of situational reasoning. We need to redefine power in a way that better balances the goals of individual and collective well-being.

For my LGBTQ friends: Gender is not binary. I'm bisexual myself so I get that. Our success in making gender choices feel less coercive does not render gender meaningless. Both nature and nurture have conspired to systemize male biases in ways that exclude feminine approaches to power. I am of the opinion that this imbalance threatens the planet and human survival. Please accept my apologies for emphasizing the extremes. I do it because I think it will help us better understand the middle.

CHAPTER ONE

MY OWN STORY

"... a very effective way to control women
is to convince women to control themselves."
—GLENNON DOYLE, *UNTAMED* (2020)

Ian and his entourage stood by the elevator doors on their way to Friday night drinks. I asked Ian once again for the sales figures that I presumed he had forgotten to share with me. Clueless, I had not yet realized that the sales figures proving the success of my test campaign might shift money from Ian's TV budget to my database-marketing budget. I foolishly thought we shared the same goal: to sell more cars for our client. On the contrary, Ian saw me as his competition. Ian lifted his keychain flashlight and shined the beam of light on my breasts, mocking me and saying, "I wonder where they are? Are they here [pointing at my left breast]? Are they there [right breast]?" I was immobilized with humiliation. Then he sneered, "Yeah, I have no idea where the sales figures are."

I felt paralyzed. Ian's protégés snickered until the elevator doors closed and then broke into roars of laughter that rose from the elevator shaft. I don't know how long I remained there, silent and incapacitated. The shock, shame, and fear temporarily disabled my brain. My reaction to sexualized humiliation was not fight or flight, but freeze, an involuntary reaction of playing dead.

That Monday our director called me into his office to say that he was very disappointed in Ian. He explained that speaking further about the event would surely make things worse. I recognized this pattern. Whenever a dominant male didn't like my behavior or wanted to dominate my work, he would shun, belittle, humiliate, or discredit me until my brain froze up or I freaked out and discredited myself. Even if I stayed sane enough to call him on it, I was silenced.

So my strategy was to pretend the incident with Ian didn't matter. Instead, I worked hard to produce better numbers that I was told would earn me a more powerful position. It wasn't long before I reported numbers so good the client decided to quadruple the budget of the database program. The director immediately hired a man to oversee the program and told me I had a new boss. It took six months, but eventually I quit. I stopped playing dead and decided to return to graduate school and study group process so I could better understand how this kept happening.

That was thirty years ago. Since then, I've had a wonderful career facilitating storytelling, group process, and dialogues that de-escalate territorial games that exclude collaborative voices. But my experiences of dominant male aggressions never let up. When my book *The Story Factor* was recognized in 2001 in the first edition of *The 100 Best Business Books of All Time: What They Say, Why They Matter, and How They Can Help You,*[1] I was one of only three female authors on the list. When the 2016 edition came out there were still only seven women on that list.

---

1 https://www.amazon.com/100-Best-Business-Books-Time/dp/0143109731

As successful as I was, I was still elbowed out of conversations, mocked, bullied, discredited, and sabotaged by dominant white males whenever they felt the need to "put me in my place." After I conducted research to document the ten tactics people use to win turf wars, I understood *how* territorial males excluded women (more on that in Chapter Six), but this understanding wasn't enough to convince dominant men to value women's points of view. It became clear that the real problem was that even women don't value their own points of view. I began to examine how that had happened in my own life.

THE POWER OF CHILDHOOD TRAINING

My mother and father argued . . . a lot. Bless their hearts, they didn't realize how unsafe their only child might feel when they yelled, raged, or shut down into a malevolent silence.

My female role models deferred to men, so I did, too. I was learning that in order to gain enough approval from men to stay in the room all I had to do was keep their secrets and play by their rules. It felt far too dangerous to trust myself to speak up when my gut feelings questioned their decisions. For example, my father told me I loved fishing. It made him happy to say so. When I was a child, he would get me up at 4:00 a.m. We stayed on the lake until I was blistered with sunburn, hungry, and humiliated by having to pull my pants down to pee over the side of the boat. I'm still not sure if I hated fishing in general or my father's approach to fishing. But I learned early that expressing my personal preferences made both of us miserable and that life was far easier when it was only me who felt miserable. My father's favorite picture of me showed me at eight years old in front of a string of bass I don't remember catching.

My father said I was an angel until I turned eleven. I remember that acting like his angel required levels of self-silencing that left me feeling crazy and angry. By eight I discovered the relief of disobedience. Saying the word "fuck" out loud out when no adult could hear bled off some of the resentments I'd stored up. The experience of having my own perceptions consistently overruled generated anger that had to go somewhere. I channeled my anger by calling out the hypocrisy of others, teachers in particular. What a joy I must have been! I apologize to all of my teachers. I was sent to the principal's office at least once a year. Today, writing this, I can see that the hypocrisy I really wanted to expose, and resolve, was my own. Scoring my father's approval required a constant betrayal of my inner voice. I learned to silence my deep desire to feel connected, to be vulnerable, and to stop chasing wins that left me feeling lonely.

Darker forces were at work, too. I was sexually abused at two and eleven and then raped at eighteen. As a result, harassment and sexual humiliation became particularly effective at disempowering me. Instead of addressing these feelings, I used bravado to mask my distress. At my summer job when I was seventeen, my boss would rub his penis against my drafting desk and talk dirty almost every day. I thought strength meant pretending it didn't matter. I was told that increasing my competence and chalking up visible achievements would earn me protection from that kind of thing.

NO PLACE FOR EMOTIONS

The people who raised me trained me, with the best of intentions, to accept that the "real world" was no place for emotional reasoning. Any emotion that indicated there might be goals more important than good grades, high scores, awards, elected positions, and looking pretty was considered a slippery slope to failure. Thus, I learned to ignore my gut so I could keep achieving visible wins.

As a child, it was easy to distinguish male narratives from female narratives, because men and women regularly segregated their conversations by gender. I remember how the women did not talk about the same things the men talked about. They talked about family dynamics, saving money, sewing, cooking, and how to convince a man to see a woman's solution as his own idea. They openly discussed how to flatter a male ego and how to avoid subjects that men don't enjoy.

Women in mixed groups could successfully discuss subjects that men enjoyed, but whenever women began to discuss "women's" subjects, the men peeled off. Suddenly there were football games to watch and hunting trips to organize. It seems to me that women are more likely to learn how to see both male and female perspectives but that men rarely stay around long enough to listen to, much less value, the reasoning of female perspectives. I genuinely believe that most men who seem to ignore women's issues fail to realize that a woman's point of view is just as valuable as a man's point of view. One of the main problems is that women integrate emotional reasoning and trust moral emotions to navigate how they define and solve problems. For this reason, women's narratives end up invisible to men who only acknowledge externally validated narratives. For instance, allocating time and resources to caregiving rarely rates a mention in men's stories about power but is often the main agenda in women's stories about power.

I am certain my father, the men in my family, and probably the men in your family had, or have, very good intentions. They don't perceive themselves as invalidating a woman's point of view as much as they see themselves as teaching her the "correct" point of view. One of the main problems I observe is that many men are bored to tears following any woman's narrative that lacks clear scorekeeping to identify winners from losers. These men genuinely believe that prioritizing scorekeeping reliably offers more accurate and useful information than an approach that tracks emotion-based evidence as a way to measure the connective quality of relationships, caretaking, and safety.

My father just wanted me to be strong and successful. From his point of view, he was teaching me how to ignore a misguided internal voice that distracted my focus away from accumulating competitive advantages. Adopting his point of view, I took mechanical drafting instead of art. By fourteen, I was regularly preparing a résumé to find my summer jobs. I studied marketing instead of psychology. I agreed to go to law school. In this way, I learned how to think like a man so I could compete by men's rules. I distinctly remember how learning to code in college upgraded my status with male students. I noticed what men treated as important and I chased the same things.

Still, I never completely shut down my internal voice. I just learned to try to make it sound "rational" by tying it to measurable wins. I learned to think in terms of transactions. In business school my advisors trained me to view life as a game and taught me to play to win. I believed that someday, if I followed the rules and kept winning, then I'd earn a chance to live by my own rules. This didn't prove to be true. Early in my career an older female politician grabbed me by the arms and looked into my eyes to deliver her warning, "NEVER, EVER do anything that might make a man's dick go limp." And sure enough, almost every time I saw a woman contradict a dominant male, she either lost or had to leave.

I had promised my father that I would go to law school, but

instead I moved to Australia. Making that move felt far easier than telling my father that I didn't want to go to law school. This became my pattern. I'd ignore my internal voice and perform by men's rules until my resentment built up enough to spin me off onto the next path that held promise. Most of the paths that promised me a voice didn't deliver. It took years to realize that none of the game-based paths could accommodate the priorities and intentions of my own voice.

In the beginning I believed that if I worked hard and produced results, I would get a chance to narrate my own life. It was a bait and switch. Each time my hard work produced results, I discovered that I still had not won a chance to use my voice. I would move on to try to win yet another game that promised my achievements would earn me a voice. While I did get to write books, my books were crafted to appeal to male preferences first. I regularly referred to myself as "infiltrating from within." My mission was to bring humanity back to places where it was missing, but without challenging the status quo to the point that I was ejected. This book is different. I'm at an age where I feel free to challenge the hell out of the status quo. I've discovered that the most honest way to narrate my own life is to reject the way toxic males evaluate me and to trust my emotions to guide me.

SWAPPING NARRATIVES

Moving to Australia in my twenties showed me the impact of changing my narrative. I learned firsthand that most of us don't even know we have a narrative until it is challenged. Growing up with people who share your narrative makes it difficult to grasp that your story isn't the only story you could use to interpret reality. When I arrived in Australia, I approached life with a common

American narrative referred to as a "work ethic." My narrative glorified hard work. I interpreted play and rest as evidence of laziness. Australian culture promoted a different narrative that valued play and rest more highly. In 1980s Australia, everyone got four weeks of vacation every year and employees were even paid an additional seventeen and a half percent above their normal income during the four weeks they were on vacation. I was shocked. But over time, I revised my narrative about hard work to include what I learned from my Australian peers.

Australians worked hard *and* took long holidays. Within my American narrative, I initially judged myself as lazy or unimportant when I took a vacation. Adopting an Australian narrative magically transformed my perspective of play and rest as vital investments in creativity, peace of mind, and quality of life. I didn't change my behavior until I changed the narrative I used to judge my behavior. Adopting this new narrative improved my self-regard, self-confidence, priorities, and behavior. That's how powerful a narrative can be. My work improved when I developed a better sense of balance. That's what can happen if you are willing to reject old narratives that cause harm. Updating the stories I tell myself about power has had similar results.

LISTENING TO A DIFFERENT VOICE

I go into all this detail for one reason. I think that if women take more time to listen to internal voices that have been systematically silenced, we can see how male narratives systematically belittle the wisdom of women's emotional reasoning. From my point of view, women's narratives seem vital to our collective survival as a species. But we need more women to trust these internal narratives before we can expect men to trust them, too.

For instance, my emotional reasoning tells me that generosity is powerful, but during my career I've had to find business goals that reward generosity with returns on investment. Unfortunately, this leads to interpreting generosity as just another transaction. One of my grave disappointments in the evolution of business storytelling has been imposed expectations of quid pro quo returns that destroy the ethic of generosity that our ancestors sought to preserve in traditional tales. When measured in the context of a competitive narrative, real generosity ends up looking like a wasted opportunity to earn something in return.

It is time to call bullshit on male narratives run amok. Contrary to what a competitive narrative might encourage you to believe, life is not a game. Pretending that life is a game favors adversarial competition in a way that discredits the idea that nature provided humans with an emotion-based guidance system to protect collective well-being from rampant self-interests. Training women (and men) to ignore nature's internal emotions is like unplugging ourselves from a vital source of survival information.

For centuries the men who invented the rules for business and politics handpicked backstories that naturally featured activities men enjoy. Heroic adventures and war scenarios determine who and what is treated as most important and cast other characters and many caretaking tasks as unimportant. Girls' stories are disdained as overly sentimental or frivolous. Dominance is featured as the best path to power while caretaking and harm avoidance are belittled as weakness or cowardice. Women who seek to avoid harm get characterized as "risk averse" instead of rewarded for their ability to avoid harm. New business practices like "just-in-time" inventory implicitly distort the wisdom of building up stores of resources "just in case" as inefficient, expensive, and unnecessary. Safety nets disappear. We are caught without enough vaccinations and without pandemic plans. Full-time focus on winning simply increases the number of losers in our societies.

I am not the only woman who feels that it is time to stop deferring to male narratives. And I am not the only one who believes that solving current world problems will require women's intuition, emotional intelligence, and emphasis on safety. The problem is that I genuinely believe the solutions we seek are invisible as long as the only contexts we use are competitive, scorecard-based war narratives. And most importantly, I'm not suggesting that we stop seeking wisdom from the well of competitive reasoning, only that we *also* need to find a way to apply wisdom from the well of collaborative reasoning. We need both. We must learn when and how to toggle back and forth well enough that the reasoning of collaborative narratives can overcome the inadequacies of exclusively competitive narratives.

Before we challenge male assumptions about power, let us first examine if it is even reasonable to sort narratives about power according to the continuum of gender.

CHAPTER TWO

STORIES WOMEN TELL ABOUT POWER THAT MEN DON'T

"As soon as you trust yourself, you will know how to live."
—JOHANN WOLFGANG VON GOETHE

After asking hundreds of people to tell "a story about a time when you were powerful," I discovered that most of the stories men and women tell are similar. Both men and women tell stories about scoring wins that offer solid evidence of tangible returns. Both tell stories about kicking ass and taking names. Both tell stories of being entrepreneurs producing multiple returns on investment, protecting profit, "killing" the competition, or winning a power struggle in competitive settings. Both tell stories about turning a failing project around, setting tangible goals and achieving them. Most of these stories support traditional assumptions that define power as the ability to dominate and control. But not all of them.

More women than men seem to suspect their ideas about power might not fit common definitions. They ask, "What do you mean by power?" I assure them I am more interested in their personal experiences of power than I am in textbook definitions.

A lot of women ask, "Do you mean at home or at work?" I let them choose, of course, but I suggest merging their experiences of power at home and work might uncover important insights we lose when we compartmentalize the methods and goals of one against the other. Some women preface their stories by offering definitions that differentiate good power from bad power. A significant number of women's stories about power openly violate traditional assumptions about power derived from centuries of male narratives, theories, and definitions. Learning how these women's narratives contrast with male-biased definitions of power might provide us with important clues as to which male-biased assumptions about power will need to change in order to integrate women's perspectives into the halls of power.

Increasing the number of women on boards, in government, and in senior leadership is only a first step to harvesting the unique wisdom that women bring to the really big decisions that decide our collective future. The second step will require that we modify decision-making habits so they better accommodate both women's and men's decision-making process, narrative points of view, and priorities.

We know how men keep women out of power, but we have failed to understand, much less overcome, the routines and reasoning behind why men feel threatened by women's perspectives. This book suggests that there are critical differences in the way men and women conceptualize power, what we think power is for, and who should have it. In this second chapter I offer three stories that represent the specific ways women's stories about power differ from men's stories. If you feel a kinship reading these stories, it's possible you already embrace a rather feminine perspective of power. If not, please take the opportunity to imagine how current decision-making routines might improve if we better integrate women's perspectives on power.

Rather than characterize these women's stories about power as out of context, irrelevant, or naïve, you may find, as I do, that a close review of these stories challenges old theories and decision-making routines that often leave women feeling powerless instead of powerful.

THE POWER TO PROTECT AND CHALLENGE ASSUMPTIONS ABOUT AUTHORITY

Robin's story about her experience of power tells us a lot about female perspectives of power. This story is one of many that showcase a woman refusing to obey traditional expectations about authority, refusing to believe lies, and persevering when stonewalled.

So this guy knocks on my door and asks, "Is your husband home?" I tell him, "I don't have a husband, but you can talk to me about whatever it is that you wanted to talk to a husband about." And it's those tree cutters from the electric company, and they want to cut my trees around the power lines. These men are obviously not arborists, they know nothing about trees, and I figure they'd just cut them all down if I let them. So I tell the red-headed white boy who seems to be in charge that I will have to supervise. His crew mostly speaks Spanish. So, one of them starts climbing up a tree and points to a branch near the wires. But what you have to know is that the poles holding up those electrical wires are leaning at an angle. If those poles were standing straight, like they should, then the electrical wires wouldn't be anywhere near my trees. So he points to one of those branches and I tell him "no." Then he points to another branch, and again I tell him "no." After a while of this I have to go inside to go to the bathroom. I came right back out, and they have cut all the branches I just told them not to cut. That red-headed crew chief (or whatever he was) acts like the guys in the trees were to blame, as if they must have made a mistake. I don't think so.

I'm getting mad at this point. It just so happened that there were two other men working on another part of my house doing repairs. I walk over and ask those guys to bring my ladder over and lean it on the tree they just cut. Then I climb up the ladder and sit on one of the branches just below the guy above me holding his chainsaw. His eyes get big like he's never seen anything like me before! And now he's stuck. They can't cut while I'm in that tree. So we just sit there. I'm not moving. It's a stand-off.

After a while one of my neighbors comes over wondering what is going on. I explain how the electric company should be straightening their poles instead of cutting my trees, then I ask her if she wouldn't mind going in my house and getting me something. I told her where to look. I had her fetch an old family Bible we keep in the house, mainly because it's family, not so much because it's a Bible. My neighbor hands the Bible up to me and I just start reading out of Genesis. I read the parts about how we are put here to take care of this earth, and how we are supposed to act, and I just kept reading. Finally, they leave.

Over the next few days, a parade of cars comes up my driveway, each one nicer than the last one. The higher up executives go the better the car they drive. These men knock on my door and want to talk to me about the trees. I tell all of them the same thing. I walk them out to look at how *far the poles are leaning over. I ask them if they think the trees would be in the way if the poles were straight. And they kind of lean their heads and I don't care from which direction you look; you can't possibly think if those poles were straight they wouldn't be near my trees. So finally, one day a really nice car pulls into my driveway and this time the man says, "Ma'am, I'm here to let you know that we will be straightening up those poles this week, and I hope you will be happy about that." I tell him, "Yes, that would make me very happy. Thank you."*

About a month later I'm telling this story to a friend who knows the CEO of the electric company. They live near each other, and at some point my friend couldn't help it and asked the CEO if she'd heard about my trees. The CEO says, "Do you mean the crazy woman out on North Road who made such a fuss over her trees?" My friend told me they had all heard of me. (Laughing.) I bet they did!"

Trust in Your Ability to Reason

First, let's look at how Robin trusts her own authority and expects the men from the power company to trust it as well. Trusting oneself when others don't is a theme that emerges again and again in the stories that women tell about power.

Rarely, if ever, do men share stories about power that begin with their need to prove that they have a right to make their own decisions. For that matter, how many men have answered a knock at the door and been asked if their wives are at home and available to talk about an important matter? And while I'm sure many of the men I've interviewed over the years value saving trees and natural resources, never has a man talked to me about saving trees as his go-to story about power.

Robin is a badass warrior woman. From the very beginning

she ignores the insulting part of the question, "Is your husband home?" Instead, she corrects the man's assumption that she is married or might defer to a husband. She goes on to demonstrate confidence and affirms her authority to speak for her household.

It is also noteworthy that while Robin rejects the assumption that she should defer to a husband, she does not take offense – at least in conversation. This strategy keeps her focused on the situation at hand. Ignoring jerks is a good power move. She does not waste precious energy on being offended, nor does she let herself be manipulated. She remains focused on her goals.

Resist Gaslighting

One of Robin's most significant power moves in this story is her refusal to pretend to believe the lie that the crew chief was not responsible for cutting the tree limbs she had explicitly marked off limits. She didn't hop up and down venting her anger with cries of "Liar, liar, pants on fire." She makes it clear that she didn't buy into the crew chief's explanation that the workers made a "mistake." She knew this was no mistake. Her references to the color of these men's skin reflects a keen awareness of the power a white man in Louisiana holds over Latino workers. When she sees that the worker has ignored her instructions, she is well aware that employees may obey a white boss man without necessarily sharing his opinions.

Robin effectively ignored the lie and stayed focused on trusting her own evaluation of the situation. She refused to let this man peck away at her self-confidence. I am reminded of the 2020 vice-presidential debates, when Kamala Harris said "I'm speaking" instead of "Excuse me" when she was interrupted.

When the crew chief tells Robin that the workers must have made a mistake when they cut her branches, he is using the age-old technique of gaslighting. This is a tool that someone claiming authority uses to try to convince a person who sees a problem the authority prefers to ignore that what she or he sees is imaginary, irrelevant, or unprovable. The purpose of gaslighting is to undermine a perceived opponent's decision to trust her own judgment and experiences in favor of false claims that sound plausible but are not true. Yet Robin remains undistracted in spite of gaslighting tactics used against her.

Stick to Your Own Narrative

Many of Robin's power moves are acts of resistance. She keeps her narrative and rejects the narrative being forced upon her. She resists the "Me boss, you little woman" narrative and replaces it with a more accurate narrative of "Me Robin, you on my land now." She trusted her own narrative so much that it created a stand-off between these two narratives. Women's stories of power often begin and end with a woman who sticks to her own interpretation of events in spite of coercive pressure. This creates a power struggle that includes some kind of stand-off as both parties decide "is this a hill worth fighting for?" In the past, authoritarians expected that a bluff was enough to back a nonauthoritarian down. They rarely had their bluff tested and so they learned that a show of intimidation was enough to win. This seems to be changing. Many of the power stories women tell now prove that a man's intimidation is wholly ineffective when you don't back down. Robin called the bluff of the crew boss. Her perseverance popped the bubble of his illusion of a threat to the point that it was the crew boss who backed down. Her power was anchored in her ability to trust her own narrative.

Prioritize a Moral Win

Protection is a strong theme in many of the stories women tell about power. Robin prioritized protecting a bunch of trees in

spite of the fact that they would never show up as an explicit as-
set on anyone's traditional balance sheet. As many other women
have done, she used her power to protect something or someone who could not protect itself. Traditional attitudes about
power usually allocate resources to protect assets that produce
economic value or to people who can return the favor. But more
women than men tell stories about using their power to protect the environment rather than profit from it. In this case the
power company calculated that cutting trees was less expensive
than straightening poles and therefore the right decision. Robin
rejected this primarily economic calculation as incomplete. She
trusted her internal calculations and prioritized a moral win more
highly than the transactional economic gain or competitive win
for the power company. The choice to value one's own internal
scoreboard over economic reasoning seems to be a distinction
that shows up in a lot of the stories women tell about power.

Construct a Shared Frame of Reference
Through the traditional lens of authoritative power, the men
with chainsaws who work for the power company hold most of
the power. And yet it is impossible to pretend that Robin, reading out of her family Bible while sitting on a tree branch, is powerless. She outlasts the daily stand-offs. As each official arrived,
she spent her time and energy to take him on a little tour so he
might check in with his own internal reasoning to re-evaluate if
the trees should be cut or the poles should be straightened. She
wasn't combative. Instead, she used her talent and energy to influence the men to see for themselves.

She invited each man to investigate if the facts he orig-
inally believed were true could be confirmed by his personal
experience. Rather than engage at the level of "I'm right, you're
wrong," she invited each guy to trust his own eyes and instincts

to redefine the problem in terms of trees that needed to be cut to poles that needed to be straightened. This strategy seems to be less about winning a power struggle than it is about expanding a smaller narrative to a larger and shared frame of reference. It is less a case of two sides competing to win as it is a process of merging multiple points of view into a bigger picture. She led each man on a little field trip to decide for himself as he leaned his head sideways to question if his initial definition of the problem might be too small or contrary to moral reasoning. Women's narratives don't cancel men's narratives so much as they expand men's perceptions to incorporate a bigger picture that often leads to different conclusions.

WORKING FOR THE COMMON GOOD

This next story, told by Kathy, illustrates how a significant number of women define power as the ability to nurture and support the community in ways that are not measured at all.

Well, I don't think of myself as having any kind of traditional power, certainly not financial or political. But in the community, I've recently started something people are pretty amazed by. It is a physical location that's kind of upcycling, or higher-order recycling. People bring things that they probably couldn't sell but somebody could use.

So we do not take clothes, we don't take books except cookbooks. We don't take furniture because we don't have room. But office supplies, art supplies, small toys, calculators, any kind of container, anything you can put things in. Wrapping boxes and wrapping paper, gift wrap, seeds and little containers to put seeds in so people can swap seeds. Magazines, small electrical tools, wire, string, pet supplies, stuff like that, that probably wouldn't be sellable but is still useful.

People bring that in, and we have volunteers who sort, clean, and organize and sometimes recycle or throw away stuff or take it to the thrift shop. I had this idea for many, many years but thought it wasn't feasible unless I was rich. Because obviously there would be some costs and there would be no income. But I talked to a family who owned a building that was sitting vacant. It was sort of an albatross around their necks. They were just having to pay taxes. I talked to them about this idea, and they liked it. They thought their father would have liked it.

I then went to a nonprofit, the president and others, and presented the idea and said, "Tell me if this is crazy." I told them about my idea, and everybody was very encouraging. They said, "No, that's a great idea. And we will help you." So then I talked to the town, a little town of 700. I talked to the county. They were both very encouraging and had good ideas and said, "We will help you in any way we can." It's right across from the recycling center. They are a big help to us and we to them.

And I have little stories, every day, when people come in. A woman came in and said, "That hobbyhorse on your loading dock would be the perfect thing for a little boy I know, who isn't going to have a very good Christmas." And I said, "Then it's yours." We had a little schoolgirl who came in and just squealed when she saw the music stand. She said, "I just started playing the clarinet and here is a music stand!" We had one man who walked in one day, took an armload of egg cartons and walked back out, without saying a word. He now knows where he can get egg cartons. Somebody else came in and brought us some packing material and said, "All I need is one sheet of black construction paper." And she got it and she left. And she said, "You just saved me a trip to town."

Define Power outside of Financial Gain

Kathy wasn't the only woman who prefaced her story about "a time I was powerful" by explicitly rejecting traditional standards of power. Many women and several men made distinctions between "good" power and "bad" power. We will go into more detail about harm avoidance in a later chapter, but basically, bad power is described as the kind of power that could control others and as a result, might coerce or harm people or nature. Good power is the kind of power that enables a community to make participative decisions. It is often described as "power-with" rather than "power-over."

Kathy's story blends all of these elements. Kathy doesn't have (or seem to want) more financial or political power. On the contrary, she defines power as her ability to spend her time, energy, and influence developing a community exchange that decreases waste, provides goods free of charge to those in need, and improves her community in ways that no one needs to calculate in financial terms on a spreadsheet. Kathy, her volunteers, the donors, the customers, the owners of the building, and the nonprofit trusted their internal judgment that this project was worthwhile without the need for a formal cost-benefit analysis.

Internal Reasoning and Unpaid labor

Kathy's story illustrates how many women track their power based on internal rankings of social and moral benefits that don't show up in most externally tracked markers of success. These women value unmeasured and immeasurable achievements like childcare, homemaking, family, and community service as being more important than money. That's probably why women's power often translates to unpaid labor. Even so, women continue to use vast amounts of time and energy achieving immeasurable goals that are not only unpaid but cost them their jobs. When women accounted for 100% of job losses calculated by the U.S. labor statistics for December 2020, it wasn't because these women didn't want to work for money.[2] Men lost jobs too, but the statistical average for that particular month illustrates how extreme the impact of the pandemic was on women. Most recent investments in infrastructure count only what can be quantified and ignore less tangible forms of infrastructure that address women's priorities. Without infrastructure that supports women's priorities like caregiving for children and elders, society loses the unique wisdom women bring to the table.

Those with a traditional approach to power might suggest that these women simply need to set up systems that better quantify these kinds of achievements so they show up on scoreboards. But how do you measure a smile on Christmas morning, egg cartons for a curmudgeon, an increased sense of belonging, or putting a lift in someone's step? Judging from how many women still allocate their power based on internal feelings they get when they imagine future benefits, it might make more sense to increase our collective faith in women's ability to seamlessly blend both measurable and immeasurable goals.

Building Social Trust by Showing Faith in Others
Most men and women possess an innate ability to sense and contribute to social systems of reciprocal generosity without

---

2 Kurtz, Annalyn CNN Business *The US economy lost 140,000 jobs in December. All of them were held by women* Updated 9:25 PM ET, Fri January 8, 2021 https://www.cnn.com/2021/01/08/economy/women-job-losses-pandemic/index.html

demanding explicit proof of benefits. We make donations, do favors, and help strangers. Yet traditional definitions of power sometimes strip us of the power to trust this innate form of reasoning. Kathy, however, knew ahead of time that "obviously there would be some costs and there would be no income." She trusted her internal reasoning that future social and personal benefits were worth her time and energy. This willingness to trust internal reasoning based on sensory cues and emotions seems vital to sustaining social trust and healthy levels of faith in ourselves and our neighbors. Social trust improves daily life by increasing collaboration, resolving conflicts, and enhancing creativity and our collective ability to provide essential security and human services.

Building systems that regenerate trust may require us to back off requiring that every decision be followed up with explicitly measured and monitored results. Trust, by definition, encourages people to make decisions without double-checking with the authorities. If evolution equipped us with emotions and internal impulses that specifically override choices limited to our own personal best interests, it doesn't make sense to obstruct the emotions that serve to sway our reasoning and decisions in ways that preserve our collective survival. Kathy's story demonstrates how often women choose to use their power to benefit the community rather than their personal bank accounts.

Merging the Contexts of Home and Work

Kathy, like many others, does not differentiate between her level of power at home versus her power at work. She is retired, but it is more than that. Many working women couldn't seem to tell a story at all without asking for a clarification, "Do you mean at home or at work?" Those who didn't ask this question largely defaulted to telling stories about workplace power. And yet, compartmentalizing different definitions of what power means at work versus what power means at home does not fully represent Kathy's holistic definition of power in this story. Dividing home and work into two separate silos of thinking falsely pits the goals and priorities of work and home into competing narratives. This is wildly inefficient. Rather than pretending that the goals of work are in competition with the goals of home and community, merging both contexts might help us make better decisions that allocate resources in unforeseen ways that benefit home and work simultaneously.

Power-with versus Power-over

The progression from Kathy's idea to its successful implementation seems weak in terms of traditional power moves. Kathy didn't come to the conversation with a clear prototype and blueprint but, rather, with an outline of an idea and good questions designed to discover and integrate shared goals. She didn't go straight to the top with a plan and a cost-benefit analysis. She had personal conversations that accumulated supporters and resources. Much like Robin, she engaged others in developing a shared context rather than delivering a fully developed context.

This progressive approach was more inclusive. The original idea adapted and changed over time as fellow community members used their own imaginations to build upon Kathy's loose blueprint. She offered an intentionally "half-baked" idea with the expectation that her ideas would be improved. Traditional expectations of authorities with power tend to reward fully baked ideas complete with a cost-benefit analysis and a plan to generate support rather than risk the unpredictability of collaborative designs. This could be rationalized with the theory that since women have less power in general, they are forced to use more collaborative procedures, but this explanation is inadequate. Many of the stories illustrate that women prefer to operate according to a "power-with" theory similar to grass roots organizing. In a later chapter we will review research that strongly indicates that this is a preference rather than an adaptation.

POWER TO PROTECT OUR NEIGHBORS

Amy Kate's story provides us with an opportunity to see how often women are required to negotiate a maze of external and internal conflicts in order to claim the ultimate power of deciding to trust one's own judgment.

> *My sister and the family were visiting, so I was outside*
> *smoking (I don't smoke around the grandbabies). I was*
> *out in my front yard so the grandbaby could still see*
> *me and not worry. I heard loud voices and realized an*
> *argument was unfolding across the street. I turned to see*
> *what was going on, and I saw the gun come out. It was a*
> *rifle, a .22.*
>
> *I yelled at my sister to get the grandbaby out of the*
> *doorway into the kitchen. And then I heard a bunch of*
> *shots, at least ten. I later learned that the shots were so*
> *powerful that some of them went through the wall of the*
> *house next door and through both walls of a twelve-year-*
> *old girl's bedroom. Thank God she wasn't in there playing*
> *at the time.*
>
> *I saw the boy with the rifle turn and run. And then I*
> *saw a boy down and bleeding in the front yard across from*
> *me. And no one was helping him. I screamed for my sister*
> *to call 911, and I ran to help.*
>
> *There were people standing around the wounded*

*boy doing nothing. I knelt down beside him and I asked
someone to get me a towel. I counted the bullet holes, and
I began to talk to him. I work in the juvenile justice system
and we see a lot of violence, so I could tell he was going into
shock.*

*I asked his name, his age. I directed his girlfriend to
help me help him. She was hysterical. I told her to "calm
the hell down" and talk to him. She kept talking about
what an asshole the guy who shot him was. I told her to
stop, to reassure her boyfriend. She needed to focus on him
right now.*

*I told him it was going to be okay, that an ambulance
was coming. I then asked him what sports he liked, and
he said "basketball." I laughed half-heartedly and said,
"Okay, you picked the one sport I know nothing about."*

*At that point, his answers began to slow. People be-
gan to drift away, and I was scared to death, but I couldn't
show it. I was kind of regretting having shown up for this
party. My sister and her kids were watching over me from
my yard across the street.*

*The ambulance arrived and they Lifelined him
out. You know, I see him on Facebook now, but he's never
acknowledged me. His mother thanked me and let me
know that he had to have a colostomy bag for a long time.
Yet, in watching both the young man and his mother on
Facebook, it's clear that their lifestyle choices will invite
this kind of violence again. But even that doesn't stop a
mom from being grateful that I helped save her child.*

*To make the story even more poignant, the boy who
shot him was one of my students from the juvenile correc-
tional facility where I work. He'd been released the year
before. After this shooting, there was a manhunt for him,*

and he ended up committing suicide rather than going back into the penal system. He was on the run after the shooting, and he killed himself with a gun in front of his mother on her front porch. Bullet to the head.

I was traumatized afterwards. It wasn't the gun itself that traumatized me, but the fact that that kid could have died on me. He could have bled out in front of me. But then, that's where the power came from.

Things like this happen at work all the time, and because of my going to the rescue of this one kid, I now rest easy in knowing "I've got this, I've got my own back." I was alone in the moments when I was applying pressure, trying to stop the bleeding. In fact, the other people all drifted to the back yard to get on their phones and text, to send pictures of the shooting. This is the world we live in now.

I was isolated in what I was doing, so I walked away with an understanding that I handled this on my own, without thought, I just locked and loaded. There was no time to analyze, to think it through critically, I just acted and did a great job. And there was power in admitting I was traumatized, too, not cold-fronting. That incident was a turning point for me. I've had past trauma that I didn't handle well. But now I know I can make better choices, good choices. I can now step out of my comfort zone and feel assured I can handle whatever goes down. I've got this.

I moved from my house after this. I had post-traumatic stress and went into counseling. I formed a good friendship with the chaplain at work, and while I'm not religious, he helped me sort through it. Most people were all "That's amazing what you did. That was wonderful." In truth, I felt bad about having gotten involved and then felt guilty about feeling bad. I understand why some

*people don't help, but that's not who I am and I'm hard-
wired to jump in and do all I can. All I saw was a kid who
needed me.*

*My newly found power shows up differently these
days. Now, I'm rebuilding my new house. Rebuilding
the back steps involves a power saw. Before I would have
been afraid of that. I would have waited for someone to
come take care of that for me. Now, I just do it. I'm no
longer apprehensive. I believe in my own capacity and
capabilities enough to know I'll figure it out. I allocate my
resources differently. If I want to know how to do something, I teach myself. I get on YouTube, look at a video,
and then I just fucking do it. If I do it wrong, I learn from
it and I figure out a way to fix it. I know I can. Seriously,
that's power.*

Choosing to Help

Few of us know for sure if we are the kind of person who would
rush in to help a gunshot victim. It depends on the circumstances. Amy Kate's decision to use her power to help this young man
was a snap judgment, based in no small part on her conclusion
that her family was safe and no one else was going to help him.
She risked harm to herself in order to decrease the amount of
harm done to a stranger.

Amy Kate had some basic first aid skills that buoyed her
confidence, but this story about power seems less about skills and
more about choosing to show up, stay present, and redirect attention from outrage and anger to caregiving. She rushed in with
positive intentions. Yet even when she began to regret "showing
up for this party," she projected enough confidence and stability
to help.

Helping when no one else is helping is a recurring theme in

many women's stories. Using one's power to help in a way that provides a good example for others translates as power in action. Rather than bark orders, this woman redirected the attention of the boy's girlfriend to see for herself how she could be most helpful. Looking at a situation from the context of "If not me, then who?" doesn't question if that help is deserved so much as it asks the question "What can I do to help?" I expect I'm not the only woman who can easily imagine being in the middle of a group of bystanders more concerned about texting than helping a gunshot victim. In this case, Amy Kate's decision to risk harm to herself in order to reduce harm to others puts a more complex spin on the common assumption that women are harm-avoidant in general.

Becoming Vulnerable in Order to Learn

Amy Kate spends a lot of time reviewing her experience and her emotions for clues to her motivation and goals. While some may call this backward review a form of rumination (often pathologized as a core weakness of women), it is a natural method for correcting mistakes and learning new lessons, especially about relationships. Statistically, it looks like men prefer to distract themselves from unpleasant emotions rather than dive in to see how deep they go. And if we are to believe the statistics that indicate men are more likely than women to be overconfident, it makes sense that men might be more likely to skip an intensive review. Certainly, the field of quality improvement has made postmortem conversations about adverse events a more normal part of decision-making. But these routines are an imposed, not a spontaneous, response. As Amy Kate "ruminates" about the event, she asks for help, deciding to be vulnerable rather than "cold-fronting" or pretending everything is fine.

Anyone who has read research professor and social worker Brené Brown's book *The Power of Vulnerability* (2012) will recognize this decision as an act of courage. As a result of choosing vulnerability, she reviews other situations where in the past she did not trust her own judgment, undervalued her skills, or avoided confrontation. She expands her new context of deciding to help when others do not as worth it in the end, in spite of what her intervention cost in terms of fear and worry. This was not about earning gratitude from the person she helped. Instead, her payoff was learning that she could trust herself to make bold choices and manage the consequences of her decisions. She derived power by evaluating for herself which goals are worth her attention and proving that her goals are achievable. This willingness to be wrong, to re-examine old assumptions, and to adapt and change is often mischaracterized as a lack of confidence when viewed through the lens of the traditional assumption that power never cedes control.

The Influence of Moral Emotions

Amy Kate's statement "I felt bad about having gotten involved and then felt guilty about feeling bad" reveals a lot about many women's experiences of power. What might sound like confusion is instead a natural consequence for anyone who acts on moral instincts to help strangers in spite of unpredictable consequences. Helping others is often a thankless job. But many women choose to help anyway. Moral emotions like empathy, sympathy, and yes, guilt, factor prominently in the process of making decisions to help people who in all probability cannot or will not return the favor. Whatever internal emotional algorithms drive women to address injustice, help strangers, and in many ways "rush in where angels fear to tread" probably seem irrational when evaluated only by economic algorithms and expectations that help is given only to those who can provide quid pro quo returns.

One of the advantages for those who cling to traditional

assumptions that limit power to pursuing only goals likely to produce returns on investment is to feel zero guilt when deciding not to help others. In fact, it seems that many of the traditional assumptions about power are designed to minimize the power of moral emotions as a force during decision-making. Trusting one's internal as well as external frames of reference makes decision-making more complicated, but it results in more balanced decisions. It seems obvious that the purpose of moral emotions is to generate helping behaviors specifically toward people who cannot return the favor. Maybe that is the point of having an internal frame of reference that drives moral emotions of empathy, sympathy, and guilt. These emotions typically override calculations of self-interest. For Amy Kate, all she "saw was a kid who needed help" and that was enough to make her decision. She did not calculate a quid pro quo return on investment.

Breaking Rules

All three of these stories illustrate what happens when a woman does not defer to traditional power structures and chooses instead to trust her own judgment, staying true to a narrative that characterizes "power-with" as a preferred alternative to "power-over." Rules and injunctions designed to clarify who has and does not have power don't mean anything to a woman who decides she is doing the right thing for the right reasons. This can seem messy, "too" emotional, and less predictable compared to cherished traditions that allocate power based on clear rules and regulations. However, after facilitating group decision-making for decades, I can attest that most of the rules that promise clarity, like parliamentary procedure, often simplify decision-making processes in ways that risk reducing the depth and quality of the decision.

It seems that no matter how long women are trained to embrace traditional ideas about power, they eventually discover that using their power to achieve their preferred goals usually breaks the old boys' rules about how power is supposed to work. It happens often enough to wonder if prioritizing masculine perspectives about power and deprioritizing feminine perspectives confound nature's efforts of supplying us with two complementary perspectives for the purpose of collective survival.

CHAPTER THREE

SEXUAL DIMORPHISM
The Evolution of Male and Female Points of View

"To hold women back, keep treating them like men."
—AVIVAH WITTENBERG-COX

As change continues to accelerate, it becomes obvious that we must pay attention to both the technical and the relational impacts these changes have on our well-being. From an evolutionary point of view, it makes sense that men and women might have naturally evolved two complementary points of view that highlight slightly different aspects of the implementation of change. If so, the benefits of allocating these responsibilities according to gender ensured that we, as a team, would cover more ground. This next story illustrates how inviting both points of view doubles the efficacy of choosing one over the other.

We went through a reorganization as a company last spring, so we started implementing the changes in like May or June. It meant that who was on what team was changing, that our reporting structure was changing, [as were] some of our systems and processes, because as the organization grew very quickly the old structure wasn't working and needed to be shifted. I was very much involved in that reorganization...I was really committed to a very positive and optimistic outlook that these changes would survive [even though] there was a lot of doubt in the organization and some skepticism as to...changes that we're making on paper.... Will they really make a difference in terms of how we function and how well we do our work?

I think the reason that I felt powerful in that process was that I was able to make sure team members felt whole. When I had new people joining my team, [I wanted them to feel] that I really recognized the value that they brought to our team, because I didn't want anybody to feel that they were being demoted in any way or that their contributions weren't valuable. I'm proud of being able to provide that positive and forward-looking outlook through what was kind of a turbulent time.

There was one team member who, because of the reorganization, joined my team and was reporting to me for the first time. This reorganization could have been perceived as somewhat of a demotion for this individual, because there were other folks that he was used to working with that he [was] no longer working with, and then he was coming under my team and focused specifically on learning. I remember sitting down with [Mark], who has been with the company for four years and has a lot of experience and is well regarded, and really asking him about what lit him up. What kind of work did he want to be doing, and what were the things that really inspired him and motivated him to do his best and learning about how creative he is and how much he wants to be involved in product development and thought leadership. It really helped me to then make sure that he had those opportunities in this role, and I feel like [he was] leveraging his skills in a way that [they] weren't necessarily being leveraged before. He had been kind of tired of being out on the road all the time with clients and not feeling like he had a chance to recharge and add his creative voice to the work that we do. That has really shifted, he's leading a new project now and is quite often involved in those kinds of creative conversations. He has specifically expressed how happy he is and how different he feels than where he was before, and others have pointed it out to me, too, [saying], "[Mark] seems really happy to be on this team, and his attitude seems to have shifted, and he's really engaged now.

My personal experience of attending to the relational aspects of implementation is that it requires me to pay close attention to the internal workings of other people based on my own internal responses to their emotional state. The relational aspect of implementation is an inside job. Exclusive focus on external technical aspects limits my ability to perceive dangerous gaps when subjective perceptions might undermine technical progress. It is a shame that competitive frameworks often distort what should be a complementary approach into a battle of wills.

SEXUAL DIMORPHISM

My friend Terri has a screened back porch where I like to drink coffee and watch the hummingbirds. The brilliant red throats and iridescent blues and greens of the male birds' feathers stimulate my attention. The brighter colors seem to suit the males' speed, agility, and aggression. I eat my cinnamon roll and wonder if the dull-colored females are less concerned about dominance because they are more interested in food. But a quick Google search on hummingbirds does not confirm my hypothesis that the males are wasting precious energy fighting instead of feeding. Male and female hummingbirds are both territorial but in different ways. According to one study, female hummingbirds perch near the feeder and wait to feed, whereas males don't display the perch-and-wait behavior. They zoom in, fight if necessary, feed, and zoom out. Sometimes they don't even feed. Sometimes they just fight. I feel an urge to translate this into meaning that the females are smarter because they know how to wait. But I must admit my bias.

Further research reveals that male hermit hummingbirds have beaks that are much straighter than the curvy beaks of female birds. The male's "dagger-like" beak offers a better tool for stabbing the throats of his rivals, while a curvy beak makes feeding easier for the females. I stop looking at the research and stuff the rest of my cinnamon roll into my own curvy beak.

The point is that it is really hard to examine the differences between males and females without imposing a competitive interpretation that frames one approach as better and the other as worse. In fact, I almost decide that watching hummingbirds is not a good way to find human analogies until I come across the term "sexual dimorphism," meaning non-sex-organ-related differences between the sexes. I like how this term removes judgments about why nature and/or nurture nudges males and females to favor different perspectives. Within the concept of sexual dimorphism, gendered specialization is simply a functional way to balance the gnarly paradoxical problem of protecting both "us" and "them." The idea that either sex's approach is better or worse only destabilizes the delicate balance of integrating both perspectives in order to protect collective survival.

SURVIVAL TEAM

Sexual dimorphism describes how males and females operate as a survival team by attending to different priorities. Like most species that exhibit sexual dimorphism, human males and females when seen up close are more similar than different. But stand way back and we have to admit there are differences. Not so much in terms of what we can accomplish, because men and women are effectively equal in terms of competence. The differences that really show up are those between what men and women enjoy, the games we like to play, and the narratives that guide our daily priorities and behaviors. If we are to understand nature on nature's terms, we must respect that in evolutionary terms, there are very good reasons for allocating gendered preferences across this continuum.

For a long time, a desire for equality at work convinced women to "prove" that there were no significant differences between men and women. During work hours, women agreed to hide such female preferences as caretaking in order to compete in ways that reflect male preferences to keep score of visible wins and status. Any woman who decided to invest her power to protect people in ways that did not offer economic returns on measurable goals had to do so on her own time, and only if she continued to meet and exceed the measurable criteria that earned her the right to sit in the rooms where decisions happen.

Should we decide to, we can choose to validate internal emotional feedback as a valuable resource for ensuring that power protects, limits exploitation, deconstructs dominance, and encourages collaboration in order to pursue long-term goals as well as short-term wins. What else but a natural instinct could possibly cause so many women to continue to perform "emotional labor" without pay other than a significant internal payoff that registers as more important than money?

The Power to Do Good

Consider this story from a woman who managed to find emotional rewards in the competitive environment of a corporate law firm.

> *I'm a corporate tax attorney at a big law firm. I've been doing this for more than five years now, but what I really like doing is pro bono work like I did at my last firm. In my current job I'm not necessarily supposed to do that work, but I wanted to and they were like, "Great, we'd love to have you help." It's been really rewarding for me; I've been able to do a bunch more pro bono than I had in the past and have been able to do some pretty substantial work. That has felt good and given me more of what I feel is more power. I'm taking control over my career and saying, "Even though this isn't exactly what you hired me to do I can do it, I want to do it, and I want to be able to use my skills that I have to help clients that more align with what I care about." I like using my power for some good and to accomplish what I want to accomplish.*

COMPETITION AND COOPERATION

The assumption that women who are averse to fighting are therefore weak and lack the talent to win has predictable consequences.

Currently, the highest power positions are more likely to be held by people who not only excel at adversarial competition but genuinely enjoy the adversarial context. This bias for adversarial gamesmanship encourages competition and work is "game-ified" to the point that peers become opponents in imaginary zero-sum games in which one person's gain seems like another's loss. Major decisions are less likely to result from a consensus including multiple points of view and more likely to become a privilege awarded to the single point of view that successfully dominates or silences other "competitive" points of view.

Francesca Gino, Caroline Ashley Wilmuth, and Alison Wood Brooks conducted a total of nine studies published by Harvard in 2015 that indicate that even when women believe they *could* win a top position if they wanted to, they often chose instead to avoid the negative outcomes they anticipated as a result of "winning." These women don't give up from weakness or a lack of desire. They make an internal decision to avoid competing in ways that undermine the goals that feel more important than winning. While research indicates that women are just as capable as men, they are less likely to see competition as the best way to achieve the goals that matter most to them. Competing to win is fun for those who enjoy it, but when it comes to protecting others, competition regularly fails to protect those suddenly characterized as losers. What this research illustrates is that a woman who might seem to "lack focus" may actually be dividing her power to attend to a much wider range of life goals than men do. Here is a quote from the research:[3]

---

3 Gino, F., Wilmuth, C. A., & Brooks, A. W. (2015). Compared to men, women view professional advancement as equally attainable, but less desirable. *Proceedings of the National Academy of Sciences of the United States of America, 112*(40), 12354–12359. https://doi.org/10.1073/pnas.1502567112

We identify a profound and consistent gender gap in people's core life goals. Across nine studies using diverse sample populations (executives in high-power positions, recent graduates of a top MBA program, undergraduate students, and online panels of working adults) and over 4,000 participants, we find that, compared to men, women have a higher number of life goals, place less importance on power-related goals, associate more negative outcomes (e.g., time constraints and tradeoffs) with high-power positions, perceive power as less desirable, and are less likely to take advantage of opportunities for professional advancement. Women view high-level positions as equally attainable as men do, but less desirable.

The fact that women find competition "less desirable" than men doesn't necessarily mean we are unwilling or unable to compete. It may simply mean women are less likely to enjoy competing purely for the satisfaction of winning when it undermines goals that seem more important.

A study from Stanford (2005) titled "Do Women Shy Away from Competition? Do Men Compete Too Much?" set up a situation in which men and women were given the opportunity to choose between two frameworks of compensation, competitive or performance-based, for performance of a simple task. Basically, the competitive frame invents a game-like battle between participants that frames other participants as opponents while the performance-based frame directs attention to each individual's personal contribution to achieving shared goals. Seventy three percent of the men chose the competitive frame versus thirty five percent of the women.[4] Women strongly preferred

---

4 Niederle, Muriel Stanford University, Vesterlund, Lise University of Pittsburgh, *Do Women Shy Away from Competition? Do Men Compete too Much? Stanford Institute For Economic Policy Research, SIEPR Discussion Paper No. 04-30 June 29, 2005* http://www-siepr.stanford.edu/Papers/pdf/04-30.pdf

the performance-based frame,[5] but why? After confirming there were no significant differences between men and women's ability to win, the researchers tested various theories as to why women did not choose the frame of competition. The researchers floated the idea that women were "risk averse" and avoiding feedback. They also offered explanations as to why men might prefer a competitive frame, perhaps due to statistically significant levels of overconfidence in men. However, none of their theories entertained the idea that these gender differences might be functional.

Instead of assuming women who didn't choose a competitive frame were risk averse, the researchers might have considered how women's choices better protect collective goals. It is possible these women have noticed how a competitive frame narrows focus and hoards resources into silos that waste what might otherwise be shared. If we expand the idea that women may reject competitive frames that endanger people and/or nature, we can better see how women who prefer collaboration over competition improve the quality of decisions even if those decisions can no longer be automated.

The Power to Take Charge to Take Care

Of course, women do not unilaterally avoid competition in every situation. Several of the stories women shared in their interviews described a strong willingness to compete, particularly when that was the only way to protect the well-being and safety of those around them. This story is a good illustration.

I had to grab power. It was thirty-six hours after the bombing of our embassy. There were three airplanes with

---

5 the researchers used the phrase "piece work" I changed it to "performance based"

three different sets of rescuers that had all experienced mechanical difficulties, which meant nobody was with us the first thirty-eight hours, and then they all arrived at the same time. More than two hundred people arrived at the same time and tried to take our power away from us. They tried to put themselves in charge.

My number two who was "acting" said to me, "Ambassador, I have to resign. I've lost control; it's total chaos out there. I'm not serving you well." And I said, "We've been bombed, things get out of control, come with me."

I walked her to the bullpen, with God knows how many people in the room. My husband (military) was there, and he yelled out, "Attennnn-tion!"

Silence in the room. I said, "Take a good look at me, I am the Chief of Mission, and nothing happens here unless I tell you it does, and if I'm not here, this is Sylvia, and nothing happens unless she tells you it does. You need to get yourselves organized and get on my schedule."

They say women take care and men take charge.
Well, in order for me to take care, I had to take charge. It is using power to do the right thing.

It may not be as much fun for some women to compete, but they will when it's important to their goals. Yet competing in order to protect others is qualitatively different from competing for the satisfaction of winning in a way that creates losers.

It just seems reasonable that both preferences make good sense from a biological standpoint. When males and females are slightly predisposed to prefer different priorities, the advantage is that mixed groups can naturally (if not gracefully) toggle back and forth between complementary strategies without inviting the disaster of choosing one over the other. Unfortunately, the impact of automating decisions with technology embedded with male biases that favor economic goals and reward competition has undermined this balance.

We endanger our long-term prospects for survival if we continue to design technological systems that prioritize competition and compartmentalization without allocating time and resources to moral dialogues about how we will protect collective well-being.

CIRCLE OF MORAL CONCERN

It is neither accurate nor respectful to judge women as being more moral than men. Rather, let's begin with the premise that men and women both express moral concerns, but that women may tend to draw circles of moral concern including people and issues that men may interpret as being outside their circle of concern. For instance, in a corporate boardroom it might seem obvious to a man that his company is not responsible for improving the working conditions of subcontractors in China. Yet it might seem equally obvious to a woman that gleaning profit from these subcontractors obligates her company to protect them.

In *The Expanding Circle: Ethics, Evolution, and Moral Progress,* first published in 1981 and updated in 2011, moral philosopher Peter Singer makes the case that altruism is a genetically based drive to protect kin and community and that as our sense of community expands, our circles expand. Factors that expand one's circle of moral concern are a belief in fairness, a willingness to share resources, and a willingness to make sacrifices on behalf of others. In cases in which women's circles of moral concern are larger than men's, women have to tolerate how individuals inside their own personal circle of moral concern are treated as "out group" and thus undeserving, expendable nonentities.[6]

Princeton psychology professor Tania Lombrozo responded to this research by making a public statement about her own circle of moral concern in a National Public Radio blog, called 'Cosmos and Culture,' which invited scientists to comment on the intersection of science and culture. Her words illustrate just how big women's circles of moral concern can get:

To Muslims and to Jews I say: You are in my circle.

To women and to people of color I say:
You are in my circle.

To members of the LGBTQIA community I say:
You are in my circle.

To immigrants and to refugees I say: You are in my circle.

To people with disabilities I say: You are in my circle.

To readers I say: You are in my circle.[7]

Our circles of moral concern have a profound influence on the way we make decisions and the way we distribute power. Everyone has some kind of circle of moral concern that identifies who does and does not deserve protection. Conflict is guaranteed

6 Opotow, S. (1990), Moral Exclusion and Injustice: An Introduction. Journal of Social Issues, 46: 1-20. https://doi.org/10.1111/j.1540-4560.1990.tb00268.x x

7 Lombrozo, Tania, *Expanding the Circle of Moral Concern*, Cosmos and Culture, NPR Nov. 15, 2016. https://www.npr.org/sections/13.7/2016/11/15/501972594/expanding-the-circle-of-moral-concern

when the circles of decision makers don't match up. Unfortunately, attempting to resolve this conflict by defaulting to the smallest circle of concern only produces moral distress for those with wider circles. For many women, the resulting inability to make moral decisions that affect a wide circle feels like the worst kind of powerlessness: an inability to protect our global tribe.

Research done in an effort to curb the nursing shortage identified that nurses often leave their jobs because of "moral distress" or the "feeling of not being able to do the right thing." If "moral distress" causes nurses to leave their jobs because they feel "powerless, anxious, and depressed,"[8] the same might be true of women who leave or choose not to compete for executive positions.

MORAL CONCERN AS A BIOLOGICAL SURVIVAL STRATEGY

Moral emotions seem essential to the survival of our species. In the book *Just Babies: The Origins of Good and Evil* (2013), about the genetic origins of morality, Yale psychology professor Paul Bloom confirms: "There are hard-wired moral universals." Even before infants can speak, they display "building blocks" of morality. Babies prefer an individual who helps to one who hinders, a helping individual to a neutral individual, and a neutral individual to a hindering individual.[9] In one research study,

---

8 *Moral Distress: What It Is And What To Do About It* Healthy Nurse Healthy Nation, Sep 11, 2017 https://engage.healthynursehealthynation.org/blogs/8/531

9 Hamlin, J. K. (2015). The infantile origins of our moral brains. In J. Decety & T. Wheatley (Eds.), *The moral brain: A multidisciplinary perspective* (p. 105–122). MIT Press. http://minddevlab.yale.edu/sites/default/files/files/Social%20evaluation%20by%20preverbal%20infants.pdf

Karen Wynn, a Yale professor of psychology and cognitive science, sat three-month-old babies in front of puppet shows with three fuzzy characters: a kitty who needs help to open a box, a bunny in a green shirt who helps the kitty, and another identical bunny in an orange shirt who slams the box shut. Eighty-seven percent of the babies who witnessed this tiny drama gazed far longer at the kind bunny, a sign of preference. Lest we think morals are all about altruism and not reciprocity, these babies were also happy to see unkind bunnies being punished.

Wynn's study illustrates how moral reasoning is a survival skill. Being born with an innate ability to read sensory and emotional cues that track who is helpful and who is harmful confirms that the capacity to tell good from bad is a vital survival benefit. This may extend to women's tendency to differentiate between good and bad power (more on that in the next chapter). New research that indicates females of the human species exhibit stronger moral identities and a larger capacity for empathy makes better sense if these tendencies are seen as a powerful survival mechanism rather than some form of cultural conditioning designed to keep women weak.[10]

Evidence shows that gendered differences in empathy have evolutionary roots in biology and discredits the argument that empathy is only a cultural byproduct driven by socialization. There are even gender differences between males' and females' affective and cognitive neural networks that increase women's levels of empathy and enhance women's social cognitive ability to explain and predict other people's actions in terms of their

---

10 Leonardo Christov-Moore, Elizabeth A. Simpson, Gino Coudé, Kristina Grigaityte, Marco Iacoboni, Pier Francesco Ferrari, *Empathy: Gender effects in brain and behavior*, Neuroscience & Biobehavioral Reviews,Volume 46, Part 4,2014,Pages 604-627, https://www.sciencedirect.com/science/article/abs/pii/S0149763414002164

beliefs, intentions, and feelings.[11] This theory is supported by behavioral studies showing that female subjects, when compared to their male counterparts, score higher on tests related to the affective dimension of social cognition, such as emotion recognition, social sensitivity, empathy, and emotional intelligence. As a result, the narratives women favor reflect a much higher interest in social and emotional factors than seems reasonable when interpreted through the battle based narratives men tend to recruit when they think about power.

GENDERED NARRATIVES MATTER

In a recent *New York Times* opinion piece filmmaker Brit Marling explains that masculine narratives interpret the idea of a strong female lead as "a man in the body of a woman I still want to see naked." Women live different stories than men do for good reasons, and Marling fights for the right to tell uniquely female stories. She continues: "Stories inspire our actions. They frame for us existences that are and are not possible, delineate tracks we can or cannot travel. They choose who we can find empathy for and who we cannot."

Most early attempts to categorize stories, including Joseph Campbell's work supporting the idea of one universal hero story, ignored female narratives. Men left home in search of risks, but women regularly risked death at home in their own bed giving birth. According to traditional storyteller Elizabeth Ellis, "it

11 Adenzato, M., Brambilla, M., Manenti, R., De Lucia, L., Trojano, L., Garofalo, S., Enrici, I., & Cotelli, M. (2017). Gender differences in cognitive Theory of Mind revealed by transcranial direct current stimulation on medial prefrontal cortex. *Scientific Reports, 7,* 41219. https://doi.org/10.1038/srep41219

is like he ignored half of the world's population." The current emphasis on hero stories leads modern storytellers to do the same.

Moreover, moviemakers and leaders who recruit hero stories only to cherry-pick the exciting bits cheat us of the moral wisdom these narratives were meant to preserve and deliver. They are missing the point: Myths, rituals, and folklore traditionally reinforced important long-term survival lessons about empathy, patience, selflessness, and trust that humans tend to forget in the short term. The original hero stories begin with the hero leaving home with less than adequate provisions only to demonstrate how a hero displays empathy as he stops along the way (usually three times) to share his meager resources with needy characters who offer no obvious way to repay his generosity. Later, when the hero is at risk of losing everything, these characters come from out of nowhere and help save the hero's life. These traditional stories illustrate the rewards of selflessness and integrity. They reinforce faith that the long-term benefits of generosity and gratitude override the benefits of selfish goals, and they pass down behavioral norms that aid survival similar to the way DNA passes down genetic information. They reinforce narratives that train our brains to focus on empathy as a way to stimulate and sustain mutual generosity. On the other hand, many modern versions of game and war narratives delete lessens of empathy in ways that encourage us to be selfish and take care of ourselves first.

I've witnessed how a new crop of storytellers often strip complicated moral narratives of long-term lessons in exchange for short-term returns. I think this shift weakens behavioral norms absolutely critical for collective survival. For instance, stories like Aladdin have lost characters and plot lines at the hands of moviemakers with a budget and time constraints. In its original form the Aladdin story in *One Thousand and One Nights* offers many more subtle and recognizable moral lessons than the movie versions do, the main one being that despite outward signs of power and wealth, the riches we value most come from meaningful relationships. And it's not just moviemakers who oversimplify moral narratives. Even with the best of intentions world leaders and corporate interpretations of storytelling promote snapshot narratives that oversimplify moral dilemmas as if they were battles easily resolved with a clear winner, rather than an endless balance between the best attributes of two sides of a paradox.

For decades, business advice essentially told women to disengage from emotions and empathy so they "could play like a man." Books warned women that "nice girls don't get the corner office" and encouraged them to lean into competitive frameworks rather than redesign these frameworks. For a long time, these strategies worked, if only because most women would still find ways to protect expanded circles of moral concern. But the increase of automated systems that only recognize quantifiable data effectively minimizes our ability to apply moral reasoning. It becomes less likely that empathy can drive decisions to prevent the kind of harm that is easier to imagine than to measure. Because it is largely impossible to prove a negative, a harm that is prevented doesn't show up as measurable. This is a fatal flaw of exclusively quantitative reasoning.

The male narratives that drive increased dependence on automated decision-making rests on the promises that groups can make faster decisions if they don't have to slow down to struggle with moral conundrums. But faster doesn't mean better. Unfortunately, there is no evidence to support the promise that mechanized "amoral" decisions can possibly keep us safe. Instead, the decreased ability to apply moral reasoning causes too many women to actively reject top jobs that don't offer enough "good" power to protect our long-term survival.

DIFFERENCES IN THE GAMES
MEN AND WOMEN ENJOY

Just about everyone enjoys playing a good game, but not everyone
agrees about what makes a game good. Every game offers some
kind of backstory that frames the goals of the game in a context of
competition and/or collaboration. Many games offer a backstory
that frames the goal as winning a battle, but not all games. Word
games like Code Name, puzzle games such as Candy Crush, and
Euro-style board games, among them Pandemic and Dead of
Winter, lean more toward exploration and collaboration. Many
evolutionary theorists consider games and the backstories they
portray as a form of play that developed in order for us to practice and learn behaviors that increase our chance to survive. The
narrative framework that builds a game's imaginary world either
reinforces or discourages attack behaviors. Research shows men
are more likely to enjoy violent video games, are more likely to
play these games for longer periods of time, and are more likely to
experience these games as immersive. One researcher found that
increasing the percentage of wins in a game kept men engaged
much longer than it did women. It's unclear if women don't enjoy
winning competitive games as much as men do or if these kinds
of games simply fail to deliver the type of "wins" women prefer.
Women's preferences lean toward games with narratives that
reward shared play and collaborative outcomes rather than sim-
ulated violence and the chance to defeat imaginary opponents.

This male preference for violent games over shared-play
games probably reflects men's preference for conceptualizing life
and work with war narratives that value high risks and high rewards. War narratives, by definition, prize invasion, speed, fighting, surprise attacks, distraction, deception, and perfidy (promising good faith without any intention of following through)

as justifiable strategies for winning. Those who most prefer war narratives tend to belittle social games like puzzles, shared play, and cooperative games as doing little more than stealing time and resources away from building battle readiness. One game designer has even insisted that a game is not a real game if it doesn't offer the opportunity to attack competitors.

It isn't an accident that misogynistic game players aggressively attacked women who openly questioned violent games that relegated females to passive roles like seductress, damsel in distress, background decoration, or as rewards. In 2014 a series of events labeled Gamergate documented a coordinated campaign of death and rape threats against outspoken female gamers who pointed out instances of sexism and anti-progressivism. These harassment campaigns continue to target gamers who suggest narratives that devalue violence. The fact that these harassers coined the label "social justice warrior" as an insult used to mock anyone who stepped up to protest their misogyny illustrates how narratives that glorify violence expect a clear winner and devalue strategies for merging divergent perspectives.

Wesley Hall Parker, a friend of mine who worked for *Game Developer* magazine, moderated sessions on women in gaming at the Game Developers Conference. She went on to make educational games for kids at LeapFrog Enterprises, where they looked at different play styles between boys and girls. Wesley says, "Women have different play styles -- just as men do. So while there are some women who like hardcore fighting games and first-person shooters, they are not as common. There is also a significant group of women (my own mother is among them) who enjoy MMO (massively multiplayer online) games like World of Warcraft. The general point is: Amazon warrior-type women exist in gaming, just as they exist among athletes. Now with that caveat out of the way, the majority of women and girls:

1) prefer puzzle-type games (Match-3, solitaire, and the like);
2) prefer casual games (less time invested / can play for shorter
periods of time / possibly because women need to be more 'in-
terruptible' than men); 3) are just as likely to be as social as men
– but in different ways – guys might be on a mic trash talking
in an online football game or hanging out with friends on a raid
(basically a war party), while women are playing Words with
Friends or similar; 4) are more likely to enjoy cooperative rather
than competitive play; if competitive it's 'friendly competition'
versus 'we are going to kill that other team over there'; 5) enjoy
games like Animal Crossing that involve collecting, farming, and
friend-making-type play patterns."

She continues: "When we were testing kids, we found the
girls were more likely to try to share their snack with any toy with
a face, while the boys were more likely to stomp on a toy or play
with it in a physically aggressive manner. Girls would sometimes
be physically aggressive in this same way if they came in with a
brother. But minus the brother, not so much. Another genre of
games that girls liked a lot was 'cooking' games. With the little
kids, both boys and girls liked the more nurturing games like
'cooking' and 'caring for a pet / raising a pet.'

Wesley's example that juxtaposes little girls trying to share
a snack with a toy the boys prefer to stomp on offers a great
metaphor for many of the situations I've watched play out in
workgroups, large and small, over the years. The problem with
exclusively competitive frames is that many men immediately
assume women's preferences are in competition with their own
preferences rather than taking the more accurate view that wom-
en want to expand single narratives to incorporate multiple goals
like making sure there are plenty of snacks for everyone instead of
ignoring snacks in favor of the singular goal of winning. As long
as these men fear that adding women's narratives will strip them

of the freedom to compete when they want to, they stomp on the idea of incorporating women's perspectives. Under exclusively competitive frames it is difficult to visualize, much less map, a path that includes both narratives without leaving competitive players with the feeling they have lost.

BUILDING SHARED CONTEXTS

Over time, the increased emphasis on quantifiable scores and competitive narratives has caused both men and women to develop a generalized disdain toward female values, achievements, and internal preferences. Evaluations of software code already deemed excellent suddenly are rated lower when the coder is given a female name. Research shows venture funders (male and female) describe young men as promising and young women as inexperienced. Men are praised for assertive approaches that earn women the dismissive title of "bitch."

This generalized disdain toward feminine narratives extends to the point that environmental concerns end up characterized, and thus discredited, as women's work.[12] These men eschew the use of reusable grocery bags as unmanly and "attribute negative feminine traits to men who argue on the basis of ethics and environmental justice—as women typically do."[13] The use of the term "negative feminine traits" illustrates just how powerfully male

---

12 Elle Hunt, *The eco gender gap: why is saving the planet seen as women's work?* The Guardian Thu 6 Feb 2020 https://www.theguardian.com/environment/2020/feb/06/eco-gender-gap-why-saving-planet-seen-womens-work

13 Janet K. Swim, Theresa K. Vescio, Julia L. Dahl, Stephanie J. Zawadzki, Gendered discourse about climate change policies, Global Environmental Change,Volume 48, 2018, Pages 216-225, https://doi.org/10.1016/j.gloenvcha.2017.12.005

narratives can undermine female preferences for collaboration, interdependence, and nurturance by portraying them as weaknesses rather than proven survival strategies.

The stakes are too high to allow this diminishment of so-called female values to continue. Today, there are obvious evolutionary advantages to drawing bigger circles of moral concern and making our decisions accordingly. But it is not realistic to expect men to come around until women clarify, validate, and honor the specific ways that female narratives about power are vital to human survival.

LATINA
woman
1st Gen

CHAPTER FOUR

FEMALE VERSUS MALE CONCEPTS OF POWER

"You had the power all along my dear."
—Glinda the Good Witch in
The Wonderful Wizard of Oz (1900), L. Frank Baum

The most obvious difference I found between men's and women's stories about power was that men almost always reported external evidence to explain what power achieved: profit, awards, staff size, and other measurable wins. Now for the most part, women also report external evidence of their power, but a significant number of women substitute their own internal criteria that places relational or moral wins as being equally important as economic or competitive wins. For these women the power to achieve a moral "win" eclipses the value of more tangible economic wins.

The Power to Care for My Child and Others
When it comes to protecting our children, women will do whatever it takes. This next story is another good example of taking charge to take care.

I have one daughter and struggle, juggling with work and the baby. For one thing, I was deprived of something I really love to do, to sleep. Finally, I met with the HR director at work, and I got hold of mothers who have similar-age children. We had a meeting with the director, and I led a team of seven women. We all had babies to nurse. The director was quite supportive in my desire for a very safe and clean environment for my daughter. Within one month, approval came for the center, and funds were apportioned, space found, and things were purchased. They consulted me, [asking] "Where do you get the best toys?" So I called a toy shop, and they have all the toys. My daughter was the first child to be enrolled. I am not a very aggressive person or anything, not too assertive as well, but at that time, I don't know, I suddenly became all those power techniques that you get from any coaching book.

A DIFFERENT DEFINITION OF POWER

At least a third of the women interviewed took time to explain that their personal definition of power was different from "the way that people usually explain it." Some women even confess that they hate the word POWER. It makes sense that women who feel oppressed by male theories of power might feel conflicted about the word. Here are some of the comments in their own words:

I'm not powerful in the way people usually mean it, meaning influence and money and important jobs and things like that, but I don't necessarily define it that way.

At work I'm a six. It's a bit of a difficult feeling toward my supervisees because I think if I'm not fair, I may actually have the power of influencing their careers (negatively), which is a bit of a scary thought.

Powerful to me is not about feeling like I'm the smartest person in the room. It's not about feeling like I control other people. It's about feeling like I'm in myself. And I'm able to share with other people to make connections. And that I feel grounded . . . that feels powerful to me.

I think truly powerful people serve a public good, be it their family, workplace, or a nation. I think power can serve across many settings. Leadership doesn't have to look like someone wearing a suit sitting at a boardroom table. It is the woman who after thirty-five years of abuse decides to divorce her husband. It is the woman at a Black Lives Matter protest, arrested, doing it anyway.

Many women felt compelled to name and reject definitions of power that focus on "influence and money and important jobs," or were set up to "control other people." When getting "arrested at a protest" against racial discrimination is categorized as more powerful than "wearing a suit at a boardroom table," it's pretty obvious that a decent number of women judge power as good or bad. They are rejecting a core assumption that power is essentially neutral, neither good nor bad, that power is amoral—something that can be used for good or bad, but is not inherently either. Avoiding moral judgments keeps things simple. When there is a war to be won, it helps to minimize the complexity of moral concerns. But for women like me, who feel obligated to pay attention to our emotional guidance systems, violence almost always feels like bad power. In fact, women often differentiate between good power and bad power, and their stories often reflect an internal pull toward collaboration, relationship building, and trust-building as good power.

> *I sometimes struggle with the word [power] because humility is something that I value a lot. I've often questioned if there's a gender component to why I struggle with that word. I think, like anything, power can be very good, and it can also be harmful.*

> *I felt personally empowered when I decided that the vision that I had was for what I could do for others. I'm a little hesitant to use the word "empowered" because it means that I am powerful. And I think of empowerment as bringing out the best in me to help others. And when I think of having power, I think of it as suppressing others. So I like the term "empowered," meaning that what comes out in me helps me help others.*

Pursuing power that exalts humility and actively avoids competing with others is a recipe for failure in many corporate situations. Women who avoid "bad power" that controls, coerces, and exploits don't end up holding the top jobs in systems that allocate power based on competitive wins. On the other hand, take a look at how this woman grappled with concepts of power and how for her being powerful came to mean helping others. Consider how contrary her approach is within a system in which power is evaluated only on measurable gains.

The Power to Take a Moral Stand

Sometimes it costs extra to do the right thing. And when that cost isn't covered many women decide to leave the system.

I've always had a desire to work in developing countries with individuals who are brilliant yet not able to manifest their brilliance. I recently worked with a nonprofit in Haiti, for a center for disabled children. An American group brought in to do strategic planning decided that some of the adult children who were being assisted by this nonprofit should be expelled from this site where they were living because they were "too adult."

These adults were aged twenty to thirty-five, and they had been living in this center for all their lives. So I pondered and pondered, and I decided that I was going to state my mind about how unfair I thought this was. I am especially attached to one man to whom I talk every Sunday. I have been talking to him for six years, every Sunday, and I still get all weepy when I think of him being thrown out on the street.

At the last board meeting, I resigned. I said, "I cannot do this. I cannot be part of this. And I will do whatever I can on the side to help this young man I know personally." And I felt so empowered that I could just say to people, "This is not the way to treat adult disabled people or anybody." I let them know that I just couldn't go along with their approach to run this center like a business and "forget the adults and they can take care of themselves. We just have to find them other places to live, that's it." So I felt so personally empowered by making a decision to say, "I'm out of here. I'm not going to be part of this group."

What Trees Tell Us about the Power of Collaboration

Let's shift our focus for a moment away from humans to trees. New research shows that trees send and receive messages via a vast underground network of roots and fungi called mycorrhizae. These deliver chemical, hormonal, and slow-pulsing electrical messages to "mother trees" that respond by redistributing water, nutrients, and even airspace to protect entire forests.[14] The unseen messages of the mycorrhizal system identify stockpiled resources, redistribute extra resources to the needy, warn of danger, support slow growth, and waste nothing. These messages naturally balance the well-being of individual trees as well as the long-term collective survival of the forest. If trees had priorities, they would never entertain the goal of being the last tree standing.

When "mother trees" send sugars to younger trees shaded from the sun they don't charge interest. Dying trees deliver their remaining resources to nurture healthier trees rather than continuing to compete and hoard resources. Trees under attack from insects send messages to the entire network so the other trees have a better chance of survival, even if the messaging tree isn't going to make it. And while there are some trees like black walnuts that try to poison the soil around them to compete with rivals, the vast majority of messages, trade-offs, and resource-sharing that happen underneath our forests are cooperative rather than competitive.

From what we've read in stories from women, it's not too much of a stretch to compare this behavior among trees with a female perspective that the power to increase collaboration is based on building strong relationships. It makes sense that, as with trees, for us humans emotions like empathy, sympathy,

14 Wohlleben, P. (2016). *The hidden life of trees: What they feel, how they communicate : discoveries from a secret world.* Vancouver: Greystone Books.

shame, and guilt also shine a spotlight on who is most in need, who has more than enough to share, and who is willing to protect the collective from danger. Obviously, these emotions run counter to systems of measurement that prioritize single wins over collective wins. But an exclusive focus on individual wins distracts us from maintaining a healthy balance.

"Girlie" Theories of Power

According to a recent *New York Times* article by Ferris Jabr,[15] when professor of forest ecology Suzanne Simard first began to research this hidden network of mycorrhiza in 1995, she "didn't receive much encouragement from her mostly male peers." She is quoted as saying, "The old foresters were like, 'Why don't you just study growth and yield?'" Simard said, "I was more interested in how these plants interact. They thought it was all very girlie." Even now, after twenty-plus years of research have "overturned long-standing misconceptions about forest ecosystems," and even though we have a new scientific journal titled *Mycorrhiza*, old, debunked methods like clear-cutting and monoculture proliferate across the globe. It is almost as if embracing the wisdom of interdependence feels dangerously feminine to the men who can only imagine power as a form of dominance.

This becomes obvious if we stay in the realm of forestry and review traditionally male-dominated strategies to improve nature, many of which eventually produce disastrous "unintended" consequences. Consider the negative consequences of clear-cutting trees or planting monocultures of only the most "desired"

---

15 Ferris Jabr, The Social Life of Forests, Trees appear to communicate and cooperate through subterranean networks of fungi. What are they sharing with one another? New York Times 12/02/20 https://www.nytimes.com/interactive/2020/12/02/magazine/tree-communication-mycorrhiza.html

species. These approaches are geared to improving growth and yield and are favored by foresters who considered Simard's views of plant interaction "girlie." Plans designed to maximize water and sunlight by clear-cutting old forests and planting only one kind of tree, like Douglas firs, in "organized" rows disastrously severs complicated networks of mutual benefit between firs and birch trees. Eliminating the birch trees severs a seasonal trade-off of carbon between the two kinds of trees that is made possible because the birch and Douglas firs have different but complementary seasonal needs.

Consider, too, how gender dynamics played out in a similar battle of man versus nature during the Covid-19 pandemic, especially in terms of how we humans responded to collective threats. Initial results implicate gendered reactions here, too, as in the male-dominated forestry strategies we just looked at. Mandates to require mask-wearing violated masculine sensibilities, and men often characterized mask-wearing as infringing on their independence (a central factor associated with masculinity[16]). One study found females to be 1.5 times more likely to wear a mask than males.[17]

---

16 Kennedy, Jessica A., Kray, Laura J., Ku, Gillian "A social-cognitive approach to understanding gender differences in negotiator ethics: The role of moral identity" Organizational Behavior and Human Decision Processes Volume 138, January 2017, Pages 28-44 https://www.sciencedirect.com/science/article/abs/pii/S074959781630749X?via%3Dihub https://www.ncbi.nlm.nih.gov/pmc/articles/PMC5364821/

17 Michael H. Haischer, Rachel Beilfuss, Meggie Rose Hart, Lauren Opielinski, David Wrucke, Gretchen Zirgaitis, Toni D. Uhrich, Sandra K. Hunter, Who is wearing a mask? Gender-, age-, and location-related differences during the COVID-19 pandemic medRxiv 2020.07.13.20152736; doi: https://doi.org/10.1101/2020.07.13.20152736 Now published in PLOS ONE doi: 10.1371/journal.pone.0240785 https://www.medrxiv.org/content/10.1101/2020.07.13.20152736v3

Male Biases in Technology

More than a few of our technological systems mimic the good intentions of foresters' methods of clear-cutting and monoculture in ways that also unintentionally sever complicated unseen networks of mutual benefit. The surge in technology designed with the male biases to trust metrics that track wins has increasingly distracted us from finding opportunities to allocate resources that pursue levels of collective well-being that are difficult to measure. For instance, social media has monetized our basic human need for emotional connection into a visible competition for "likes." Tallying up how many of our online "friends" hit the "like" button distorts what used to be emotionally driven exchanges of reciprocal concern.

Taxing formerly free exchanges of human attention with ads and loss of privacy naturally reduces generosity and weakens ancient behavioral norms of reciprocity we now call social trust. For instance, when algorithms based on keywords invite me to "connect" based on automated criteria, it betrays the old-fashioned expectation that an invitation to connect was a compliment. These automated connections make me feel less like a friend and more like a commodity. Building a "platform" in this way inhibits both parties from engaging in the kind of intimacy that generates trust.

Focuing only on "growth and yield" emphasizes power strategies that are just as short-sighted as clear-cutting trees and creating monocultures. Strong negative emotions against sacrificing individual wins for collective wins create a bias that undermines networks of interdependence. As we continue to lean on rational logic and intentionally exclude emotional logic and moral reasoning normally associated with female perspectives, we risk our collective well-being. It is now much easier to see that the truly rational approach to power must incorporate a way to strengthen, not weaken, mutual relationships.

Not for Women Only

Women in general seem to show more interest in interdependence and connections than men. These observations are in keeping with a Harvard-sponsored meta-analysis of thirty-three studies that found a significant gender difference in the strength that moral identity plays in male and female identities.[18] According to the analysis, any randomly chosen woman is approximately 66% more likely than any randomly chosen man to have a strongly internalized moral identity. Many of the studies indicate females are less tolerant of unethical behavior, and one particular study shows that females experience a stronger emotional aversion than men to actions that cause harm. The study found that while there are no differences between men's and women's cognitive abilities to foresee outcomes, women were more empathetic with people negatively impacted by those outcomes.[19]

Before women become too quick to reserve what we deem to be good power as an exclusively female trait and mistakenly characterize ourselves as the world's harm-avoidance experts, it's important to note that there are plenty of men ready and willing to recruit a collective narrative when it comes to power. Unfortunately, many women don't seem to realize how often we discourage men from expressing empathy or showing moral concern.

18 Kennedy, Jessica A., Kray, Laura J., Ku, Gillian "A social-cognitive approach to understanding gender differences in negotiator ethics: The role of moral identity" Organizational Behavior and Human Decision Processes Volume 138, January 2017, Pages 28-44 https://www.sciencedirect.com/science/article/abs/pii/S074959781630749X?via%3Dihub

19 Friesdorf, R.; Conway, P.; Gawronski, B. (2015). Gender Differences in Responses to Moral Dilemmas: A Process Dissociation Analysis. Personality and Social Psychology Bulletin, 41(5). http://www.spsp.org/news-center/press-releases/gender-difference-moral-judgments-rooted-emotion-not-reasoning-study

Brené Brown points out in her book *Daring Greatly* (2012) that women who easily embrace vulnerability in themselves can be slow to reward vulnerability in men. When women mindlessly expect men to be dominant and fearless, they overtly encourage battle narratives that frame men who avoid harm as weaklings.

Raising sons to be more like women sounds good in theory, but it can feel risky in practice. Still, if we genuinely want to redefine power so that it adequately represents feminine preferences for mutual gains as well as masculine preferences for competitive gains, we will have to figure out a way to improve the status of men ready to act "like women," at least when it comes to avoiding harm. In a world turned upside down by a pandemic, economic turmoil, and increasing risks from climate change, it becomes clear that at this point in our story the avoidance of harm is not a weakness but a survival strategy. With good intentions of eliminating bad emotional decisions, we have nonetheless minimized moral emotions that might trigger better decisions that protect instead of exploit, and that share rather than hoard resources.

The Power to Be Kind

Performance measurements that exclusively emphasize efficiency often undermine the time and effort it takes to be kind to coworkers.

> *My director was away for a long time, so I was pretty much working on her behalf on a lot of things. I was renewing staff contracts and giving people promotions or influencing their promotions and working with the human resources department. Then I realized that the way a lot of people's lives could be bettered, in terms of their working conditions, depended on me. It was very humbling when people come and really open up to you and tell you their stories,*

their highs and their lows and their frustrations. It is very
humbling. The feedback I got from the majority of them
was that they trust me and that I'm a very approachable
person. So I have never known that I had power, but I
kind of found myself in a very powerful position at that
time, or at least I had what I thought power was.

The Danger of Using War Narratives

I must confess that the extreme popularity of heroes slaying dragons is a pet peeve of mine. The metaphor of slaying dragons is too
often used to reduce paradoxes into imaginary battles that make
one side always look good and the other always look evil. Bless
our hearts, our craving for clarity has meant that our storytelling
has begun to misrepresent life's conflicts as battles that can be
won decisively. We seem to forget that what we characterize as
a dragon almost always represents the shadow side of a couplet:
The dragon of fear limits desire, the dragon of selfishness stalks
tolerance. But these are not simple zero-sum challenges in which
someone wins and someone loses. Desire also limits fear, and too
much tolerance impedes self-care. Long-term solutions require
balancing these opposing forces rather than vanquishing one side
or the other.

I am reminded of the old facilitator trick when we ask members of a group to pair up and grasp hands for sixty seconds to see
how many points participants can score by pulling their partner's
hand toward them across the middle. After sixty seconds most
pairs, faces red with effort, report scores of less than ten, but a
few clever partners who decide to collaborate and swap turns
score up to sixty "wins" each. Embracing paradoxes (good of the
individual and collective good) is much more efficient than treating a paradox as if it were competition between right and wrong.

Yet examples like traditional military training show tactics that are designed to inhibit empathy and pre-empt moral judgments in efforts to increase speed, focus, and kill rates. After the famous combat historian S. L. A. Marshall estimated that only 20% of World War II soldiers actually pulled the trigger in fighting situations, the military developed new training to automate behavior and desensitize soldiers to their emotions in ways that increased the ratio-to-kill up to 85% during the Vietnam War. The ratio-to-kill continues to "improve." A friend's son, a young West Point graduate, sat me down to explain the advanced tactics used to improve this ratio-to-kill. It soon became obvious this young man did not suffer from the same internal alarms I felt as a result of our discussion. He was quick to point out that on a battlefield my caution would translate into weakness that might result in greater harm down the line. I could have pointed out that inhibiting empathy might be just as harmful down the line, but he had already been trained to discredit my line of reasoning. Then again, I couldn't blame him for being trained to think in terms of war narratives. We have lionized men who win for so long that we have stolen the dignity of men who choose collective well-being over personal gain.

Without a doubt, if winning is the only goal, it is highly efficient to eliminate empathy. Moral restraint only slows things down and also stimulates empathies that discourage easy wins and inhibit economic exploitation. Competitors increase their speed when they eliminate the need to slow down and check their moral consciences. Focus improves immediately when you avoid integrating multiple perspectives and time spent anticipating conflicting goals. Power brokers who are happy to let the chips fall where they may save time and energy that might otherwise have been spent investigating, anticipating, and avoiding "unpredictable" negative consequences. If your world view is one of competition, any desire to improve the well-being of people we don't know personally in ways that are impossible to measure looks like a sure recipe for losing.

In many current power structures, fighting to win is better rewarded than preserving stability, distributing resources, or protecting strangers. I have been told point blank by several powerful men that viewing life from a collective point of view is straight out "boring." But we can't afford to let powerful men continue to treat the planet as a gaming arena for imaginary wars. To "win at all costs" or acting as if "failure is not an option" do not promote the collective good. As long as war narratives control our perceptions of power, any desire to avoid harm and protect strangers looks like a weakness. Sharing resources with someone who can never pay you back is no way to win a war. In a war scenario, only a weakling dodges the harm of battle.

The expansion of war narratives to health care and economics ultimately discourages collaboration, discredits empathy, and blocks emotional reasoning from influencing behavior. It is imperative that we reverse the trend to discredit and minimize moral concerns as inefficient or weak. Unless we find a way to reinvigorate moral emotions, we could easily win our way to vanquishing our chances of collective well-being. On the other hand, if we succeed in dialing down our reliance on war narratives in order to prioritize collective survival, our opinions about what power is, what it is for, and who should have it will change. In the collective narrative, large-scale efforts to reduce harm by providing free health care and reducing poverty by redistributing economic resources will look far more heroic than heroes who slay dragons that probably have something important to say.

The Power to Share

If Stephen Hawking was right and greed and stupidity are our greatest enemies, we need new strategies for rewarding selflessness and wisdom. And if nature decided to equip women with a peculiar sensitivity to moral goals and selflessness, now is the time to capitalize on that sensitivity. Whether you are male or female, if you ache with concern over our collective future, you are receiving moral emotional messages loud and clear. It is up to us to make these messages more visible and turn them into action.

Here is one woman's reflections on what it meant to respond to the call to help others:

> *I was invited to do training with other communications specialists. I was allowed to present the work I was doing to others. I was being asked to talk about what I'm doing and share something. My experience matters and can help others do their work better. It can guide them. It was very satisfying and empowering, and I felt very powerful. Not in a negative way powerful, "Here I am, look at me." But just incredibly honored and empowered to show that, you know, to be part of the community and contribute to the community on that level.*

CHAPTER FIVE

HOW WOMEN'S NARRATIVES CHANGE THE STORY

"As a woman I have no country. As a woman I want no country.
As a woman, my country is the whole world."
—Virginia Woolf

Let's reconfirm that when it comes to *abilities*, men and women are effectively equal. The differences between what men and women *can* do are minor, if they exist at all. But men and women are not the same when it comes to our preferences. Just as we prefer different kinds of movies,[20] it also seems that we *prefer* to use power for different kinds of goals. Second, we don't want to overstate what are slight gender differences. If we were to plot women's and men's movie preferences along a continuum from "all about relationships" to "all about blowing shit up," the bell curves would mostly overlap, except for the extremes. Many

---

20 Wühr P, Lange BP, Schwarz S. Tears or Fears? Comparing Gender Stereotypes about Movie Preferences to Actual Preferences. Front Psychol. 2017;8:428. Published 2017 Mar 24. doi:10.3389/fpsyg.2017.00428 https://www.ncbi.nlm.nih.gov/pmc/articles/PMC5364821/

differences are not huge over the spectrum, yet studying extremes is the best way to understand the push and pull of preferences in the middle. We will only make sense of the male/female tug of war over power when we concentrate on how often these preferences mischaracterize the other side as the opposition.

The Power to Influence
Women's stories regularly valued influence more highly than control. The problem with control is that most communication is one way (top down), whereas influence depends on keeping both lines of communication open. When women's ideas about power center on responsiveness and dependability, then having too much control threatens to cut off communication.

> I would say I'm very dependable. And everybody in my family has grown to rely on me over time. They take my views seriously because I give my advice and I give my views after due consideration. I don't really consider myself to be powerful. For me, power is not about intimidating people. That makes me very uncomfortable. The kind of power that attracts me is knowledge. I've always been on a lifelong quest for knowledge. My office recognized this, and our leadership began coming to me to seek opinions, get advice, and saying we must ensure that we are involving you or consulting with you as we do other work. So that makes me feel powerful. My colleagues also come to me, and I've done quite a bit of coaching with them. I can see that I've had a very positive influence in other people's lives, and this makes me feel powerful, like, "I actually have power to influence people."

WOMEN'S POWER PREFERENCES

Below are two lists that summarize random sets of twenty true stories each gender told when asked to tell a story about power. Take a minute to review both lists to see if you can tell which list summarizes the stories men told about power and which one summarizes the stories women told. If you can tell a difference just by reading these few summaries, it doesn't mean you are guilty of genderism. It simply means that you also notice that men and women tend to use power to achieve slightly different goals. Take a minute to judge for yourself. Which list came from women? The first or the second one?

List #1
Forgave someone and moved on; blocked another person's access to resources; interpreted someone's dream for them; won a book contract; increased TV invitations from 1 to 4-5 opportunities a month; earned an invitation to contribute to a proposal; acted as a gatekeeper to control information; went above my boss' head to get another job; delivered a great presentation even though my slides didn't work; shifted student's "mentality" to include new choices; got accepted into grad school; interpreted cultural and technical information to others; testified against abusers; anticipated needs and prearranged logistics; got a promotion from managing 0 to 160 people in six weeks; refused advantages based on privilege; turned down unethical request; earned status by association; my student won an award; obtained high value item for free

List #2

Mentored an employee to success; established child care at work; increased wages for underpaid employees; instigated a memorial to commemorate a bombing; arrived first to help a shooting victim; helped my community get a grant; tracked a lost relative to facilitate reconciliation; won a pro bono case; went above my boss' head to get another job; prevented another person from misusing power; evacuated a hospital ward during a flood; negotiated a raise for my employee; protected a child; facilitated an aid package to help a poor country: proved discrimination to win more of a government contract; improved working conditions for women at work; implemented a more ethical accounting system; traveled in spite of a severe handicap; started a nonprofit; exposed a lie

If the second list seems more female somehow, your instincts are accurate. The first list illustrates that men's stories were more likely to cite achievements with external evidence, such as an increase in staff, access, control, or profit, whereas women's stories cited internal as well as external evidence of power in action. Women told more stories about protecting people who can't pay them back. They seem to value their power to nurture, protect, and connect as much as they do external evidence of their achievements and rewards.

These findings offer a clue as to how and why women use more of their time and energy to provide unpaid "emotional labor." Sociologist Arlie Hochschild coined this term in the 1980s to describe time and energy spent managing one's own emotions, but the term has since been recruited to describe the unpaid time and effort women expend in order to keep those around them comfortable and happy. This unpaid work of remembering birthdates, giving care, cooking, and keeping the cultural traditions that make life feel meaningful is unpaid, because these actions fail to produce material wins on visible scoreboards. The fact that women continue to use their power to perform emotional labor in spite of the lack of extrinsic rewards further illustrates how women value internal criteria as equally important as external criteria. Otherwise, why do women continue to do it?

Widen the Circle and the Irrational Looks Rational

In the early 1970s, the psychologists Amos Tversky and Daniel Kahneman introduced the term "cognitive bias" to describe systematic but purportedly flawed patterns of judgment and decision conundrums. Promoting the idea that rational responses would, by definition, maximize personal gain, researchers have now categorized what might well be evolutionary patterns of collective reasoning as irrational. Behavioral scientists have now identified almost two hundred "irrational" patterns they consider to be cognitive biases, i.e., errors in judgment. However, the real error might be limiting our calculations as to what is/isn't rational based on individual or organizational self-interest. We know at a gut level that unregulated competitive pursuits of self-interest inevitably overexploit collective resources. We've been talking about it since 1833, when the British economist William Forster Lloyd pondered the problem of unregulated grazing on common land. A 1968 article in *Science* magazine by the ecologist Garrett Hardin went on to describe this phenomenon as the "tragedy of the commons." Selfish interests eventually overgraze and threaten the well-being of the commons. So from a collective point of view, curbing the overexploitation of resources is more rational than mindlessly maximizing gains.

In order to avoid individual strategies with predictable consequences on collective well-being, humans developed behavioral norms and emotional payoffs that reward these "irrational" choices (self-restraint, generosity, harm avoidance) by ensuring that these behaviors provide more emotional meaning than material gains after a certain point. We cultivate traditions and stories to celebrate "irrational" sacrifices like random acts of kindness so they motivate us to put the welfare of others over our own once our needs are met. From the perspective of protecting collective well-being, nothing could be more rational than to know when it is time to forfeit personal gain in order to secure collective well-being.

As an example, one cognitive bias called "loss avoidance" is the tendency to avoid giving up something when doing so might mean gaining something better. From a ratio-based perspective, risking loss is the price of gaining more and gaining more is the goal. But this ratio-based analysis cannot duplicate the meaningful emotional perspective of knowing how much is enough. When it comes to addressing climate change, it is highly rational that once an individual or group has enough of what they need, they hang on to what they have and let other people gain what they need. While this runs counter to the logic of consumerism, the psychological payoff of avoiding loss once you have enough is strong enough to override the promise of even more. The wholesale labeling of loss aversion and other biases as irrational threatens the network of unseen checks and balances sustained by emotional (moral) reasoning.

Every attempt to judge emotional payoffs according to ratios of utility misunderstands the nonlinear nature of emotions. The emotions that drive caretaking are a good case in point. Many women would be loath to perform emotional labor that was translated into externally visible reward systems like reviews or bonuses. Imagine if families posted reviews and scores for emotional labor—say, three stars for Tuesday night's dinner or one star for parenting. Metrics like these would drain the joy out of cooking all day for Thanksgiving as well as hinder the courage it takes to tell kids "no" when that is not what they want to hear. There is a real danger that quantified scoring and competitive frameworks could invalidate the power of emotions like love and trust that currently fuel emotional labors vital to our collective survival.

Extrinsic rewards will never support the kind of reasoning produced by intrinsic motivational systems. Not only is it impossible to predict accurately and measure what moral decisions might gain for future generations, but quantifying "acceptable" levels of harm only makes it easier to justify doing harm as a cost of doing business.

The implicit assumption that women who are "irrationally" averse to loss and harm and are therefore weak or lacking talent has predictable consequences. The highest power positions continue to be held by those who risk, win, and enjoy adversarial competitions. It also ensures work is increasingly designed to encourage competition and is game-ified to the point that peers become opponents. The long-term result is that major decisions are less likely to result from a collaboration between multiple points of view and more likely to result as a privilege awarded to whomever successfully dominates or silences alternative points of view.

Internal Guidance Systems
Just because women are more likely than men to split their power, time, and resources to pursue invisible rewards as well as visible rewards does not mean that women don't enjoy competitive wins and external rewards as much as the next guy. Instead, it simply means that women are less likely to live off of an exclusive diet of external motivation. Women and men with large circles of moral

concern crave, desire, and long for internal payoffs as much as external payoffs. Consider this extended list of the plots women recruited to define power.

Developed a curriculum to teach kids about climate change; returned to school; ran for office; called out sexual harassment; corrected an injustice: turned away from a desire for revenge; reduced racism; survived abuse; helped an intern succeed; wrote an article that resulted in legislation against violence; spoke publicly about an unpopular truth; kept family together; refused to intimidate others; won regulatory approval to test a drug; disobeyed an order to be silent; gave someone a second chance; got my husband to help with childcare; refused a job until gender issues were prioritized; unloaded a freeloader; prevented the destruction of my trees; dressed a two-year-old child and got to work on time; made sure team members felt whole instead of demoted; mentored a woman to speak up for herself.

As you may imagine, the results of speaking up, reducing injustice, risking exclusion, or walking away on principle are more likely to decrease external rewards than increase them. Yet these women (and men who also value collective perspectives) still report these behaviors as power-in-action. It is a powerful feeling to know when you have gained enough and can turn your attention to protecting others. Women steadfastly continue to use their power to manage things that aren't being measured. We trust our hearts to measure the power of correcting an injustice, turning away from revenge, risking unpopular topics, speaking up in spite of personal risk, giving second chances, bargaining for childcare help, or checking in to see if the people on your team feel whole.

Split Attention

If you consider that many men seem to navigate their worlds according to a dominant guiding star of external feedback while women calibrate their journeys according to two guiding stars, one of internal feedback as well as one of external feedback, it's easy to understand a lot of the criticism men level at women. Men living in a world that only registers external wins might see no valid reason why women willingly lose for a greater cause, fail to negotiate top dollar, fail to exploit opportunities (or people), and give time and energy away with zero returns on investment. Recognizing these differences also helps us better understand how a man who is free from constant intrusive reminders about the emotional well-being (or lack of well-being) of others could easily use up all of his energy winning at work instead of saving time and energy to shop for and cook a healthy dinner for his family.

This mismatch of focus accounts for men who describe women as difficult, unfocused, or wishy-washy. Women who experience emotional fulfillment protecting the weak are unlikely to chase wins that exploit the weak. Women may be consistently tracking emotional payoffs as data for internal scorecards that are invisible to many men. All of which makes women who respond to internal emotional triggers look like bad team players to men focused only on visible wins. To men, women seem too emotional, and to women, men don't seem to be emotional enough. To women, men may seem to ignore important emotional data to the point that they seem narrowly focused, lacking empathy, and over compartmentalize solutions that cause more problems than they solve. A man who was trained to disassociate from emotional truths might even seem immoral. Certainly, paying exclusive attention to external contexts diminishes one's ability to incorporate such internal contexts as one's moral conscience.

The Legitimacy of Internal Context

Cognitive neuroscientist and neuropsychologist Elkhonon Goldberg invented a "cognitive bias test" in the 1990s that unexpectedly yielded significant differences between males and females. When I first ran across Goldberg's results (published in 1994), I came to an interpretation rather different from the one Goldberg described in the first edition of his book *The Executive Brain: Frontal Lobes and the Civilized Mind* (published in 2001). It's important to state up front that Goldberg doesn't at all agree with my interpretation. But I think the story of our interactions illustrates how male biases can belittle female biases in ways that turn into discrediting and disdain.

The idea behind Goldberg's cognitive bias test was brilliant. He designed a test that reduces context so that neuroscientists could measure how our brains, specifically the frontal lobes, sort out decisions when denied meaningful context. Without context we risk making really bad decisions, and without shared context nations find it impossible to achieve the broad agreements necessary to make hard decisions on issues such as climate change. Because context is so important, Goldberg set up an experiment that denied test subjects context to see what happened next.

Here's how it worked: Subjects were shown a card with a shape followed by two more cards, each also with one shape, and given these instructions:

"You will see cards with different designs. The designs may vary in several respects. You will see a card at the top and two cards below. Look at the top card and choose one of the two cards below that you *like the best*. There are no "correct" or "incorrect" responses. Your choice is entirely up to you. Please, try to choose quickly."

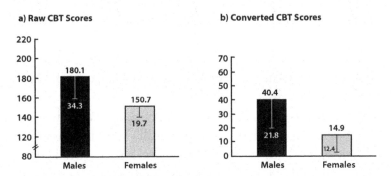

*Means and standard deviations for raw (**a**) and converted (**b**) CBT scores in strictly right-handed healthy subjects*

The subjects are told that there are "no correct or incorrect answers" and that the "choice is entirely up to you." However, when Goldberg tabulates results he treats the first card that subjects are told to ignore as a contextual cue. In later summaries he calls that first card a "target card." After seeing the shape on the first card, men were more likely to choose cards with shapes that reflected a relationship to that first shape. He called their choices "context-dependent." Women, on the other hand, felt free to make choices unrelated to the first card. He called these unrelated choices "context-independent."

He interpreted the results according to his narrative that context is a function of external cues. This led to his supposition that men are more likely to pay attention to context, whereas women seemed to ignore it. If I could possibly agree that only external contexts matter, that would be that. But it wasn't. My research tells me that women draw contextual information from internal cues that feel just as important to us as external cues. What seems unintentionally sexist about this test and Goldberg's interpretation of the results is that he seems blind to the possibility that female subjects aren't immune to context, but they often treat internal cues as equally valid as external cues when making decisions.

To be fair, Goldberg was not expecting gender differences. Nor was he expecting me to show up as a student in the summer class he was teaching on Cape Cod in 2005. But I saw his research in a completely different light, and I wanted to ask him if he could see what I saw. Specifically, what I saw was that women who seemed to "ignore" the target card were more than likely substituting their own context—say, a strong preference for circles—instead of the "clue" they were told to ignore. I see these women as just as "context aware" as the men who chose to use the target card as their context; women drew on an internal preference, such as a fondness for specific shapes, as their context. I wanted to see if he might be interested in my point of view. I suggested that if I was taking this test and he told me that the first card didn't matter, I would feel free to choose whatever shape I liked best for my own internal reasons. If I liked circles better than I liked triangles (even if a triangle was on the first card), I was free to choose circles over and over again. I was free to use my internal preferences and ignore the not-a-target target card.

I was a little slow to pick up that Goldberg was not interested in hearing my alternative interpretation during class. He suggested we speak after the class. I waited. He met me outside, but once I started talking, he pointedly made a phone call and ignored me while I tried to explain. I would stop to wait, and he would motion me to continue even as he was talking to someone else. I suppose he was simulating what he thought I had done to him during class. I am left to assume that his desire to even the score (as he saw it) was more important to him than whatever curiosity he might have felt about why I was so eager to talk with him.

This was not the first time I had run across male reluctance to address the importance of subjective internal criteria. When men accuse women of bringing up subjective and thus (to them) irrelevant issues it may be that they simply don't value internal cues. Could it be that simple? If men's narratives discredit internal criteria women can't ignore, little wonder that it's hard for men and women to get on the same page.

How We Tend to Explain These Differences

Once I raised the point about internal cues in his class, there was a small discussion before I was dismissed out of hand. It is important to note most of the men and women in the class agreed with Goldberg, even to the point of naming the women who chose shapes inconsistent with the target cards as afflicted with the mental pathology of perseveration—the act of repeating a response long after the "appropriate" stimulus is gone. From their point of view, choosing all circles was obviously a sign of meaningless repetition. It is interesting to note that perseveration is considered typical of autism. Greta Thunberg's activism may be a good example of a situation where perseveration isn't as mindless as some might think. In spite of criticism from men who obviously think Greta's repeated warnings about climate change are inappropriate, she perseveres. She certainly seems more attuned to an overpowering internal impulse framed by intrinsic moral reasoning than short-term economic reasoning. And while she attracts attacks from men who disagree with her, her power to change global conversations about climate change owes everything to the way she values her internal sense of right and wrong over external pressures.

Hopefully, you and I can learn from her example. At the very least we can anticipate the shape and form of attacks we will attract when we demand our rights to use power in order to protect humanity.

When Having Power Feels Like a Straitjacket

It all boils down to money (big surprise). After thirty years of trying to identify the core conflict at play, I'd like to propose that dominant male narratives tend to focus resources on strategies that earn power to dominate as much of the collective as possible, whereas female narratives about power siphon off resources to protect the collective in ways that neither dominate nor monitor. From a "power-over" point of view, diverting resources to invest in the unquantifiable promise of long-term collective well-being seems weak, unprofitable and, worse, it distributes gains to strangers with zero promise of quid pro quo. Well-intentioned attempts to invent measurable sustainability goals further reflect the male bias against prioritizing intrinsic, emotion-based judgments. Excluding women who trust intrinsic emotional reasoning or forcing them to limit themselves to quantified gains has led to chronic underfunding of collaborative strategies that might otherwise have addressed climate disaster, decreased poverty, and better managed mass migration. Limiting investment to protect the collective proactively also led to a stunning lack of preparation for the Covid-19 pandemic.

A recent study published by the World Economic Forum now confirms what many have suspected: "Being female-led provided countries with an advantage in the current crisis." The global call for more women leaders is a direct result of the success of Jacinda Ardern, who led New Zealand through Covid-19 with strategies that resulted in zero cases; Angela Merkel in Germany, who demonstrated the role of empathy as an organizing principle; and Norway's Prime Minister Erna Solberg, who held a dedicated press conference specifically for children in which she used her power and resources to explain to them that it was okay to feel scared. I can't imagine that a decision based exclusively on quantified returns on investment would include comforting children first. Yet all of these women made good decisions based on complex moral instincts that defy measurement.

Women leaders apply different priorities because women view power through a different narrative lens. As a result, women allocate resources toward goals that seem irrelevant when viewed through male narratives about power. News reports continue to document how female leadership proves better suited to protect collective well-being. What is not so easy to see is how increasing the number of women in leadership will require concrete changes to broaden strategic goals, the way money is allocated, and the way we measure progress.

The failure to anticipate that women recruit different narratives to define what power is, what power is for, and how we define success consistently undermines our best efforts to increase the number of women in positions of power. As you can see from the material I've collected for you in this book, this will only be possible if big systems are willing to reconcile the way male and female narratives about power prioritize goals and allocate resources.

If I'm reading this right, increasing the number of women in power will require a dismantling of toxic competitive frameworks that discourage collaboration. Recruiting more women to power will require that we rearrange priorities to include moral goals and emotional reasoning. As a result, budgets will shift from always chasing wins to include protecting people. There will be unpredictable scenarios that challenge some of the cherished assumptions baked into traditionally male-biased power frameworks. It can only help to try to anticipate and prepare for the divergent perspectives women will integrate into traditional power structures. This book offers some ideas on how, rather than ending up blindsided by our differences or sabotaged by power struggles, we might peacefully anticipate differences on our path to building a healthy mix of male and female narratives in time to protect our collective survival.

How We Interpret the Differences between Male and Female Stories

My hope is that reading this cross section of women's stories about power illustrates how many women evaluate collective well-being as the goal of our narratives when thinking about what power is and what it is for. Most of these stories were gathered pre-Covid, but they give us an idea of why female leadership during Covid was more successful than competitive male narratives. Yes, it's messy, but I'm betting the stories validated much of what you already intuited. Men tend to score power based on observable gains, while women often score intrinsic gains as just as important as material gains. Male narratives often discredit emotional reasoning as being unstable and unreliable to the extent they defer the kind of moral reasoning required to protect the collective.

The obvious goal is to find the ever-moving sweet spot between protecting the survival of individuals and protecting the collective. However it happened, it seems as if nature or nurture evolved "female" perceptions that power is to be used to protect the collective, while "male" narratives tend to interpret power primarily as the ability to dominate the collective. Challenging centuries of "power-over" theories to make way for methods and routines that support "power-with" theories is bound to rock the boat.

The next chapter seeks to anticipate the tactics that dominant males might use to continue to discredit, shame, and exclude women. Again, we will discuss how these tactics undermine women's self-regard to the point women have learned to discredit our instincts preemptively. My hope is that by validating women's "different" perspectives on power we can build enough strength and solidarity that will enable women's narratives to achieve the goals of protecting our species and our planet.

Why Not Eliminate the Focus on Gender Altogether?

Is gender that important? If you identify strongly as female or male it is. Even if you live somewhere in the middle of the spectrum, gender still offers us a way to identify the two ends of the continuum in a way that acknowledges that both perspectives are equally valid. While our society increasingly embraces gender fluidity and expands our freedom to choose the traits and physical presentation that best match our chosen gender, this trend does not make gender irrelevant. In fact, it seems to do the opposite. Rather than collapsing gender stereotypes into androgynous nongendered composites, these new freedoms encourage all individuals to explore and adopt the gendered traits that suit parts of their chosen male, female, or nonbinary identities.

Thankfully, gender has become less coercive, but it is no less relevant. We can support the idea that gender is central to most people's identity without judging them as choosing the wrong gender. We can eliminate disdain for those who reject traditional gender identities at the same time we elevate the idea that both gender preferences offer complementary evolutionary benefits. It is worthwhile to consider that evolution developed male and female preferences to bridge the tension between two vital survival strategies: competition and cooperation.

CHAPTER SIX

WHAT TO DO WHEN COMPETITIVE GAMES THREATEN COLLABORATIVE PREFERENCES

"A woman has to live her life or live to repent not having lived it."
— D. H. LAWRENCE, *LADY CHATTERLEY'S LOVER* (1928)

Norway started a gender-quota movement in 2003 by instituting a 40% female quota for corporate boards. Since then, Spain, Israel, Kenya, Portugal, and Germany have followed suit with their own quotas. In 2020, California became the first U.S. state to enact a threshold for female representation in the boardroom. These strategies to increase gender parity are a start but are not enough. While gender quotas definitely help, they don't address the way that competitive narratives usurp collaborative narratives. Inviting women to participate in board-level decisions on the condition that they operate according to male-biased competitive narratives defeats the benefits of including women in decision-making.

Harvard researchers[21] in India describe a specific issue: "Even though the newly appointed female directors were more educated and likely to have more political experience than their male peers, they were less likely to be appointed to key board committees, even when the researchers controlled for previous board experience." They concluded: "Quotas are not enough to ensure actual governance reform in internal board processes."

Yoshiro Mori, former Japanese prime minister and head of the Tokyo committee organizing the 2021 Summer Olympic Games,[22] gave voice to an unspoken male narrative when he said, "If we increase the number of female board members, we have to make sure their speaking time is restricted somewhat, [as] they have difficulty finishing, which is annoying." As you might imagine there were calls for his resignation (he eventually stepped down), and he admitted that his wife and daughter gave him an earful when he got home. His example further reveals that inviting women to male-biased boards is not enough to prevent competitive narratives from discrediting the methods and priorities of collaborative narratives.

In the case of Yoshiro Mori, his perspective caused him to conclude that when several women spoke up about the same issue, the women were displaying excessively competitive behaviors. I wasn't there, but my interpretation entertains the possibility that these women might have been trying to support each other. It's relevant that the core conflict was probably the concern that hosting the Summer Olympics of 2021 might be unsafe for the population of Japan. This is a classic example of how the

21 Ruth V. Aguilera, Venkat Kuppuswamy, and Rahul Anand, What Happened When India Mandated Gender Diversity on Boards, Harvard Business Review, February 05, 2021 https://hbr.org/2021/02/what-happened-when-india-mandated-gender-diversity-on-boards

desire for achievements and the desire to avoid harm are treated as mutually exclusive or, worse, unrelated. This tactic of accusing women of talking too much in order to discredit them is one of ten territorial games I discovered when gathering stories about turf wars in work situations.

Competitive Narratives Drive Territorial Games

While Angela Merkel initially led Germany's successful approach to contain Covid-19 infections, by 2021 re-election concerns by her peers shifted attention away from narratives about protection to less complex narratives that prioritized short-term election wins, deferring concerns for safety for later. This shift led politicians to oust Merkel and delayed another needed shutdown. As a result, cases of Covid went up in Germany in the spring of 2021. This shows how often avoiding harm ends up at the bottom of the agenda the minute a group's story shifts to short-term wins.

In today's world the "territory" for which game players compete is no longer defined exclusively by geography. The new kinds of territory that competitive players seek to dominate include information, communication channels, and relationships. By controlling these, game players control which narrative determines perceived priorities and problems. What's more, while women succeed in making structural changes that decentralize control, welcome multiple narratives, and nurture relationships, competitive game players feel threatened and see all the more reason to treat women with collaborative preferences as enemies.

It's important for women to understand the nature of competitive game playing. Once we recognize certain behaviors as being part of a competitive game, we are less likely to be blindsided by them. Since competitive narratives conspire to frame alternative narratives as opposition, we have to be careful to avoid responding in kind. To avoid being sucked into this competitive frame and responding with tit-for-tat responses, detachment is key—detachment denies game players the rush they crave.

Understanding the Emotional Reasoning behind Territorial Games

At the extreme, hypercompetitive narratives invent doomsday scenarios that portray collaborative approaches to such issues as health care and climate control as forces that will dismantle economic progress, help people who "don't deserve" it, and disfigure capitalism. The emotions stimulated by imagining these disastrous scenarios incite competitive players to feel justified to use warlike tactics to discredit collaborative strategies as dangerous losses, both irrational and naïve. They force competitive and collaborative narratives to compete instead of finding strategies that balance both approaches.

To be clear, all narratives evolve from emotional reasoning. It's just that competitive players are less aware how their emotions are amplified by scorekeeping, because their scores are ratio-based. Highlighting wins and losses then overstimulates certain emotions like desire, greed, pride, anger, hate, disdain, and fear, while discrediting emotions of love, empathy, and sympathy as losing strategies. I worked at a consulting firm that displayed "billable hours" for each employee where we could all see who had the highest numbers. Our boss no longer needed to manage us, he just sat back and let the numbers on the board whip up our competitive instincts. The approach increased billable hours but didn't make for a very collaborative environment.

The Battle for Budget

Few events illustrate the limitations of competitive reasoning better than a budget meeting. These meetings are often approached as if they are a battle for limited resources. Thirty years of consulting has taught me that most participants implicitly agree to lie about how much budget they actually need. People tell me they calculate budget needs and then add 30%, or they double the number, or inflate the number in some other way because they expect that everyone else is doing the same thing. When I ask why they hide the true figures, most people report that they don't feel like they have a choice. Once I was hired by someone in the Pentagon to help facilitate a budget meeting for a work group assigned to care for soldiers' families and housing. I decided to run a little experiment to see if I could change the current battle narrative long enough to change the results of their budget meeting. While using poetry may not be a viable strategy for most people, I recount the story here because it illustrates one way to reveal conflicting priorities without invalidating either.

I first affirmed that in a war-fighting situation, competitive narratives help us to ignore pain, unplug empathy, and limit our focus to winning at all costs. For eons military groups have used speeches, rituals, and music to summon up a blood thirst for winning. As an example, I recited a speech from the pre-battle scene in Shakespeare's *Henry V*:

> Once more unto the breach, dear friends, once more,
> Or close the wall up with our English dead.
> In peace there's nothing so becomes a man
> As modest stillness and humility:
> But when the blast of war blows in our ears,
> Then imitate the action of the tiger;
> Stiffen the sinews, summon up the blood,
> Disguise fair nature with hard-favour'd rage;
> Then lend the eye a terrible aspect;
> Let it pry through the portage of the head
> Like the brass cannon; let the brow o'erwhelm it

As fearfully as doth a galled rock
O'erhang and jutty his confounded base,
Swill'd with the wild and wasteful ocean.
Now set the teeth and stretch the nostril wide,
Hold hard the breath and bend up every spirit
To his full height.

By the time I finished fists were clenched and the group was pumped up with testosterone. I heard several huzzahs. Not a few looked like they were doing impressions of the Hulk. I may have been one of them. It is an exhilarating narrative. They knew this emotional state well from decades of military training, and it didn't take much to evoke it. We had fun debriefing the behaviors it stimulated. However, I told them, my goal was to switch the narrative from treating this budget meeting like a battle to a more collaborative narrative based on mutual obligations to share resources in ways that were best for the soldiers and their families, even if it required some sacrifice (aka losing). I explained we needed different emotions to make good decisions and asked permission to share a few excerpts from the Billy Rose poem "The Unknown Soldier." I invited their imaginations to conjure up different scenes and a more collaborative narrative.

There's a graveyard near the White House
Where the Unknown Soldier lies,
And the flowers there are sprinkled
With the tears from mother's eyes.

I stood there not so long ago
With roses for the brave,
And suddenly I heard a voice
Speak from out the grave:

"I am the Unknown Soldier,"
The spirit voice began
"And I think I have the right
To ask some questions man to man.

"Are my buddies taken care of?
Was their victory so sweet?
Is that big reward you offered
Selling pencils on the street?

"Did they really win the freedom
They battled to achieve?
Do you still respect that Croix de Guerre
Above that empty sleeve?
...
"I wonder if the profiteers
Have satisfied their greed?
I wonder if a soldier's mother
Ever is in need?

"I wonder if the kings, who planned it all
Are really satisfied?
They played their game of checkers
And eleven million died.

"I am the Unknown Soldier
And maybe I died in vain,
But if I were alive and my country called,
I'd do it all over again."

The emotional shift in the group was palpable. Emotions

of humility and gratitude for soldiers who made the ultimate sacrifice reframed our perspectives. This story shifted the plot from protecting budgets to protecting soldiers and their families. Many knew soldiers who had died in the line of duty. I asked them to imagine what questions those who died might ask from their graves about how their budget decisions would impact the care provided to living soldiers and their families. Empathetic reasoning deprioritized competitive goals. Enough of them stopped protecting silos to reprioritize shared goals and shared budgets. Changing the narrative changed the emotions and changed the outcome of this meeting. It was akin to a spiritual experience, wholly intangible but profoundly moving.

When you are in charge of a meeting like this, you, too, can use storytelling or other forms of art to first validate the emotions and perspectives of those bringing competitive narratives in order to earn the right to offer alternative narratives that emphasize shared goals, inspire mutual sacrifices, and build a big enough picture to reveal the harm win/lose reasoning poses to collective well-being. Many women (myself included) have been trained to keep our predictions of harm to ourselves based on past experiences.

Internal Conflicts
Those of us who try to promote collaborative narratives, goals, and methods often find ourselves defending our reputations and ideas from the attacks of competitive players. These "opponents" tend to brand us and our ideas as being misguided, inefficient, or weak. If we buy into their judgments, we get defensive and perpetuate competitive behaviors that do more harm than good. By mindlessly responding to attacks in kind we undermine our own ideals of collaboration. This is not to say that there aren't times when we must respond in kind, but the best-case scenario

is to de-escalate and stay connected.

In competitive terrain, it is considered fair play for a player who considers you an enemy to convince you that you and your ideas are so irrational and unreasonable that you should stop trusting your own judgment. In order to weather this kind of gaslighting, we must upgrade our confidence in our own perceptions before we can generate enough power to encourage others to trust us. Granted, it's hard to trust yourself when competitive narratives portray your worldview as inefficient, irrelevant, or, worse, counterproductive. For many women (myself included), these confrontations even trigger oversized fears from earlier traumas. To be honest, I went into therapy in order to finish this book, and sometimes I wake up feeling nauseous and afraid because I know speaking up for women's narratives about power will invite attacks.

Convincing those in power to allocate resources to pursue moral outcomes will require high levels of solidarity. It is up to all of us to summon the courage we need to ensure collective narratives become at least as important as competitive narratives.

Learning how to inoculate ourselves against the attacks that defending a collaborative narrative can provoke requires good strategies to stay sane, stay present, and maintain forward progress. It's important to remember that avoiding harm is nothing to be ashamed of. You must also keep in mind that unpacking the emotional origins behind cherished competitive scoreboards may make you a target. Strong women are attacked, undermined, belittled, and marginalized.

So many of us have been trained to betray ourselves when attacked that we need to practice standing strong. Learning to trust yourself begins as an inside job that you can expand to support others. Mental rehearsals help. Sometimes, I use my imagination and practice how to set my eyes, my posture, my tone, and my timing to express my unwavering faith that power at all levels should protect collective well-being.

One of my touchstone memories was formed at the same budget meeting I mentioned above when a combatant male general later yelled at a female lieutenant, "WHY DON'T YOU JUST GROW UP?" Her answer was priceless. In a tone simultaneously cool and warm she asked, "I don't mean to be disrespectful, but could you be more specific?" That is what a woman who trusts herself sounds like: unflustered, calm, and strong. Compared to the female lieutenant, the male general sounded like the bully he was.

In one of the first stories you read, the woman who went to the aid of a shooting victim said "I felt bad for getting involved and then I felt guilty for feeling bad." Navigating two narratives naturally produces internal conflicts. I think that's why so many women feel conflicted about the very word "power." I suspect this is why dominant men label women willing to compromise as "wishy-washy." If you feel embarrassed about having mixed feelings, please let that go.

The Power of Ambiguity

Mixed feelings prove you care about both competition and collaboration. This woman's story is a good representation of what that looks like in action.

> I've got both the position (I head a unit) and I participate in organizational level discussions, strategic, and all that. So my input is usually taken into account. I feel appreciated, and I think I make a difference at the highest levels . . . there are some things that will not be finalized without my input. That's what I do.
> We had this project where it needed to move from

research into the farmers' hands. Nobody had ever done this before. This now came down to me. And the donor said, "organize a team, [you] be the chair of that team, and organize outreach activities to ensure this is regulated well, it passes the regulatory process, receives public support, and we get approval." And so I chaired that particular committee for a while. And the end result is we did get the approval. And the donor was quite happy. Wait, I have a feeling that does not show power. No, it doesn't sound powerful all of a sudden.

Ambivalence is the natural result of balancing the dueling goals of individual gains and collective well-being. In the story above, the word "power" activates an internal struggle between two narratives: we did this versus I did this. Once women redefine power as a function of both collaborative and competitive narratives, embracing these ambiguities need not activate self-doubt and should instead become a mark of complex thinking. We've been fed the myth that embracing ambiguity is a sign of a lack of focus. While this is technically true, rigorous focus on competitive goals is a dangerous form of tunnel vision. Embracing the ambiguity of contrasting yet complementary narratives is a required capacity to find the sweet spots between both individual and collective goals. Most creative solutions will be found in the gray area in between. And heads up, it is likely that these creative solutions will be so well-adapted to local conditions and emotional undercurrents that they risk appearing to be random or "out of control" when evaluated by competitive standards of speed and efficiency. So I doubt making progress will make things easier, at least initially. Perseverance will be required.

Common gaslighting tactics convince women that we are crazy, wishy-washy, too weak, or too strong. Unfortunately, these tactics have been very effective, though they are not true. Anyone, male or female, who toggles back and forth between competitive and collaborative goals is trying to balance an irresolvable paradox: self-interest and collective wellbeing.

Toxic men will continue to marginalize and belittle women's points of view. Some men get off on dominating strong women. Our challenge is to find a healthy way to manage our emotions at the same time we nullify the games. It's not easy. De-escalating territorial games takes a lot of self-discipline. There are many times when you have to give someone a second chance to do the right thing. Every now and then we are clever enough to say the perfect thing, but more commonly de-escalating territorial games requires resistance and perseverance. It will take a massive amount of faith in ourselves and each other to build dual narratives. Personally, I persevere because I have faith in you and all women, as well as the men who share our perspectives. The stakes are too high to give up now.

Ten Territorial Games

Twenty years ago, I asked hundreds of respondents to share "true stories about a turf war you personally witnessed." Ten patterns emerged, and after my book *Territorial Games: Understanding and Ending Turf Wars at Work* was translated into Spanish, Portuguese, Swedish, German, Chinese, Japanese, and Taiwanese, I was surprised to learn from readers that the same ten tactics occur in every culture.

While some people admire these games like a playbook for winning, most realize that the games decrease the flow of information, cut off relationships, and unplug empathy. Our ability to anticipate these games rather than being blindsided by them creates a shared immunity to gaslighting and games.

BEFORE CONSENSUS

Territorial games begin long before decision-making occurs. Social media has made it much easier to spot attempts to control narratives so they downplay predictable negative consequences for the collective and overemphasize the benefits of short-term wins for a select few.

Occupation Game

Back when territory was primarily geographic area, strategies to control and occupy ground were more tangible. Occupation meant constructing houses in coveted territory, building walls, instigating wars over minor encroachments, and displaying warnings, say, by beheading intruders and putting their heads on display. Today, however, competitive players seek to control the "territory" of information, relationships, and communication channels. The games are similar but less tangible, and the majority of players are the kind of men (and women) who seek to dominate positions of power with a single competitive narrative.

Territorial game strategies seek to control conversations with the specific intent to marginalize collaborative narratives and discourage collaborative emotions. These strategies thrive by promising rewards for competitive tactics and threatening danger for those who don't play to win. The fear of losing a promotion or even one's job is enough of a deterrent that many of us fail to run experiments that might prove that these perceived threats are illusions.

Response

Build up the numbers to increase the "territory" held by those who support collaborative narratives. Recruit collaborators. Show up even when you aren't invited. Create channels of

multiple knowledge

communication that welcome multiple narratives. Show care for women who are attacked and join them to help them hold their ground. Expose the harm of "winner takes all" reasoning. Continue to prove by example that diversity increases creative intelligence. One woman's story provides a great example of how to respond to these kinds of games:

Diversity

creative intelligence

> *I think my power really comes more from persuasion and having the ability to speak very persuasively and take some risks in the conversations. Like telling new leadership when they've gone too far, legally and policy-wise. I have been able to take risks by looking high-level leaders in the eye and saying, "You're really screwing up and let me help you."*

Intimidation Game

When a competitive player is threatened by what you say, they will do whatever it takes to shut you up. Sometimes they blame "how" you said it when the truth is that they feel threatened by "what" you said. Others use visible cues to threaten, perhaps by clearing their throat loudly, raising an eyebrow, or pushing back from the table. Some competitive players recruit even more aggressive tactics, such as invading your physical space or threatening harm to your status or safety. Sexual harassment is a terribly effective form of intimidation.

Some players flip the game by accusing a woman of being intimidating. In most cases, when a man tells a woman that she is intimidating it's a strategy to cause her to doubt herself and back down. This happens more often when men are so emotionally triggered by the fear of female anger that they actually do feel attacked.

Response

I admire women who can stay calm enough in the face of intimidation to keep others calm. Melinda French Gates, Kamala Harris, and Stacey Abrams are role models. Intimidation is particularly hard on women with PTSD (there are so many of us). Developing the ability to hear/see/feel the threat while taking a deep breath and staying sane and clear-headed often flips the focus back on the bullying behavior. The story of the female lieutenant earlier in this chapter is a good example. It's also important to remember that intimidation is often actually a bluff on the part of competitive game players.

Likewise, choosing to stand beside any woman who is being intimidated usually exposes these threats as bluffs. Since intimidation works best in the shadows, increasing awareness often changes behavior. Increasing the level of psychological safety in groups reduces intimidation tactics. In a collaborative framework, intimidation tactics lose status. Speak up to protect anyone who is being bullied.

DURING DECISION-MAKING

Once a workgroup moves toward decision-making, the games can intensify. If a game player feels like they are losing control of the narrative, they move on to controlling who gets to talk and devising intentional distractions.

Filibuster Game

The filibuster game is similar to the occupation game. Monopolizing airtime decreases the chances for anyone to question dominant competitive narratives. The tactics range from overtalking, pushing collaborative issues to the bottom of written agendas so time runs out, and quoting a woman in a way that reinterprets her intended message into something ridiculous. Overtalking is both a recognized political ploy and an unconscious response for competitive players who want to control a conversation. "Mansplaining" is also a form of filibuster. Often unaware that they are running off at the mouth, many men who feel threatened are only aware that when they are talking and you are not, it feels much better than trying to listen to what you have to say.

Response

Former Secretary of State Madeleine Albright, when asked about the one piece of advice she'd give to women, said, "Interrupt." When we don't interrupt, bullies gain confidence that they have the right to control the dialogue. A consensus about time limits may protect marginalized voices. Putting collaborative issues at the top of meeting agendas can help, too. There will also be times when you can step in and summarize a filibusterer's point, verify that what you heard is what he meant to communicate, and then ask to hear other perspectives. Another tactic is to ask for a show of hands of those who have not yet spoken and suggest that they speak before anyone else talks again.

Camouflage Game

When a group begins to question assumptions cherished by competitive players, a camouflage game player knows he can distract attention away from consensus with a "what about?" question. Unsettled by perceptions of lost ground, game players propose disastrous "what about?" questions that emphasize an opposite extreme view of whatever paradox you are trying to manage. They invent slippery-slope hypothetical scenarios that reframe compromises as dangerous. Dire predictions of lost incentives, exploitation by free riders, and loss of control can divert a meeting minutes from consensus into a wild goose chase. Groups have a natural tendency to chase wild geese when they fear the consequences of closure, so this technique is particularly effective to prevent or delay a consensus that requires compromise. Tough decisions that require self-restraint, sacrifice, or self-discipline are most susceptible to being delayed by triggering fears.

Response

When you can, point out in advance that tough decisions naturally inspire groups to indulge in avoidance strategies. Name any fear-based distraction for what it is, then validate, calm, and guide the conversation back to closure. You may need to fully narrate the predictable scenarios the group will risk if they continue to avoid tough decisions.

DURING IMPLEMENTATION

Coercive tactics don't always stop after a group reaches a consensus, and just because a decision is made does not mean it will happen. Some game players consider themselves clever when they agree up front only to undermine progress later. One woman describes the sort of competitive player who never gives up and who has no concern for the common good.

> I am very clear on what I think is bad power. I look at
> [unnamed] and he is a very powerful man, but it's not due
> to any authentic connections. His power comes from his
> family, from money, and his absolute willingness to spend
> money to get what he wants and his willingness to remove
> anyone who is in his way. He doesn't care who he has to
> dump in order to get what he wants. That kind of power is

evil, selfish, and malicious. It is a kind of power that is in no way good for anyone.

Invisible Walls Game

Competitive players may agree in public to a collaborative initiative only to later place roadblocks to prevent it from happening. When conflicts are treated like wars, misdirection seems justified. Sometimes all it takes is a disdainful tone to act as a dog whistle to encourage noncooperation among the competitive troops. There are a million ways to set up roadblocks to prevent or distort progress.

Response

A great deal of gaslighting is involved in this game. One of the crucial aspects for understanding and overcoming invisible walls is to understand the endless energy and effort competitive players will spend constructing these walls. Once a group has characterized decision-making as a prize to win rather than an opportunity to collaborate, they are willing to unleash the power of "control the narrative" campaigns that oppose more complex strategies that recruit multiple narratives. While collaborative players avoid the assumption of ill intent, it may be necessary to compete on their terms to minimize the damage of invisible walls. If you suspect insincere agreements might lead to these invisible walls games, your best strategy is to undermine these walls before they are constructed. I can't think of a better example of an invisible wall than voting rights restrictions portrayed as preserving integrity--when they are in fact designed to exclude minority voices.

Strategic Noncompliance Game

Some competitive players don't bother with invisible walls. They intentionally advertise agreement to collaborate in public as a tactic to buy enough time to undermine that agreement in secret. Lately, this seems to happen more often in the political arena as extreme competitive players advertise they will punish anyone who decides to collaborate or act in a bipartisan manner. The pressure increases the fear of collaboration to the extreme. It doesn't take long for trust to evaporate in these situations.

Response

The best tactic is to openly investigate hidden reservations that might otherwise fuel strategic noncompliance. If you can, invite people to share personal stories that represent the power of collaborative alternatives. This reveals the level of emotional commitment group members feel in a way that can expose future noncompliance. Take a bit of time to imagine "worst-case scenarios" that reveal the consequences of unseen resistance. Negotiate frequent and early milestones as a part of group agreements. Regularly affirm compliance with a personal conversation instead of relying on technology. Follow up early and often. Explicitly ask allies to report noncompliance as early as possible.

Information Manipulation Game

When I first researched these games in the nineties, I had no idea that this particular game would turn into an industry. Back then I heard stories about competitive players who withheld information (like my colleague Ian failing to find the sales reports, as I report in Chapter One), doctored statistics, or misrepresented their intentions. But today, people are paid to invent and promote false information specifically to manipulate strong emotions like outrage and disdain. The more visceral the information, the better it sticks. Accusing public figures of child pornography, ritual murders, or other salacious acts triggers adrenaline rushes that were once reserved for rare occasions of real danger and can become addictive. A steady stream of titillating information simulates meaningful connection for those who feel chronically unengaged. Framing every day as an epic battle gives meaning to their lives and alleviates boredom. The high stakes drama eclipses the drudgery of solving complex problems with discipline and shared responsibility.

Response

My hope is that technology platforms will continue to take responsibility for reversing disinformation campaigns. Employee actions help. Boycotts help. Still, waves of blame and outrage have proven strong enough to turn family members against each other. People with collaborative goals are more likely to resist the urge to repost misinformation that demonizes some "other" as their enemy, but competitive players thrive on it. Those who are lost in competitive narratives may even view the failure to repost outrageous warnings as a weakness. My personal strategy is to increase the intimacy of my relationships enough to share information that might expand circles of moral concern. I try to support good journalism and generate social proof by sharing personal eyewitness accounts of collaboration at work. I help fund arts that amplify compassion and activate moral emotions. We need to create our own factories of true stories that prove the value of collaboration.

MANIPULATION OF SOCIAL STATUS

Whenever you hear the words "This isn't personal, it's just business." They usually precede a threat to your social status if you continue to defend your point. Over the centuries, we can plainly see that business is affected by personal relationships. The assertion that "this isn't personal" is used to justify all kinds of harm. "Someone offering help doesn't need to claim that "it isn't personal." Competitive players blinded by illusions that scoreboard wins absolve them of the personal impacts their business decisions impose on the coworkers, the unemployed, the environment, or global emotional health cut themselves off from the need to acknowledge empathetic perspectives. These last three territorial games deliver personally hurtful forms of marginalization that demoralize, disconnect, and isolate at the same time they protect themselves with plausible denials designed to blame and shame those they wish to exclude.

Shunning Game

This game shows how often public humiliation, mockery, patronizing statements, or ridicule are used to silence collaborative voices. Some game players set up town meetings or other "public" hearings for a time or date that guarantees to exclude other voices. Collaborative thinkers are particularly susceptive to the threat of exclusion and isolation. "Doxing" individuals who have exposed wrongdoing by publishing private information about them online in order to facilitate harassment is a new form of shunning. Shunning activates deep survival fears of the harms that result from being cast out of the tribe. This game is designed to overwhelm a truth speaker with so much shame and fear that she is silenced.

Response

If you are a collaborative thinker, prepare in advance for shunning behaviors. Build your resilience by processing a healthy, sane response to shaming behaviors. Naming the behavior is a healthy response if it helps you shine a light on moral goals that evaporate the shame and fear. Stepping up to protect others from shunning increases the likelihood that they will do the same for you. Share stories about how to best manage our natural emotional reactions to shunning. Accumulate feelings of belonging by tending to personal relationships with people who affirm the value of collaborative narratives.

Powerful Alliances Game

Bringing in a heavyweight can make divergent voices feel small. Cronyism activates territorial behaviors from unexpected sources. At times powerful alliances can elevate into a virtual lynch mob. This is another game that has been flipped backward. Now that collaborative voices must call out those who do harm, powerful alliances have learned to counter-accuse moral objectors as creating "cancel cultures" as if they are the voices excluding divergent opinions. This is another form of gaslighting that sounds plausible enough to encourage competitive players to make alliances and target those who promote collaborative narratives as an enemy. It is easy to feel outnumbered. Name-dropping those who carry out threats is used as a warning.

Response

The good news is that some of the richest and most powerful people in the world now support collaborative narratives. Examples include "the giving pledge," initiated by several billionaires to make the "moral commitment" to give away most of their money. As collaborative alliances build allies across multiple networks, the norms and goals of alliances shift. We are gaining converts. In the meantime, it can be very effective to believe and behave as an equal to those who protect competitive narratives. Steady eyes, relaxed posture, and self-confidence go a long way to shift the dynamics of those who treat their status as a competitive win.

Discrediting Game

This is an ancient game amplified by the exponential reach of social media. Smear campaigns, false accusations, shaming photos, and outright lies seem like fair play to a competitive player who sees you as a threat. Disdainful responses to the efforts of the #MeToo movement displayed the range of labels used to discredit those who seek equality and inclusion. Truth speakers are discredited as revenge-seeking, angry, irrational, weak, too emotional, improper, ridiculous, unattractive, too butch, too femme, or lacking likability. All forms of trolling on social media fall into the category of the discrediting game.

Response

It is easy to repeat the platitude that only sticks and stones can break our bones, but we know that words still do damage. I expect to experience the discrediting game as a result of writing this book. I think it is predictable for anyone who threatens the dominance of competitive narratives. Since we are all imperfect, many attacks are based on a grain of truth that makes them sting. If we haven't already come to terms with our own flaws, we risk disappearing into a shame cycle. If I get a chance, I will acknowledge my flaws in the proper context. But the primary strategy is to refuse to engage. Much of the time, engagement only amplifies the attack. Defending someone else who is being attacked can increase the circle of people willing to protect you when it happens to you. The long game is to enrich collaborative narratives about power to the point that the danger of dehumanizing marginalized voices with discrediting tactics is obvious.

De-Escalating Game Playing

While the goal is to avoid game playing, I admit there are times when I've chosen to go toe-to-toe with a misogynist. But on these occasions, I escalate a conflict only slightly, just enough to prove I could fight to win but prefer to offer a second chance to de-escalate. It amazes me how often people will respond to a second chance.

Once the CEO of a company was stonewalling me by refusing to meet in person before I facilitated a day-long meeting with his top executives. His boss, the chairman of the board, had hired me but would not be attending. The CEO wasn't thrilled about spending a whole day making a plan to avoid territorial games, because he liked territorial games. From experience, I knew a personal conversation was the best way for me to pre-empt the subtle tactics he might use to undermine my credibility. I had observed him playing games like discrediting, intimidation, and strategic noncompliance, so my best bet was to anticipate and head off these behaviors by discussing them ahead of time.

As I said, this CEO stubbornly refused to meet with me before the event, not even for breakfast the day of the event. We were still on the phone when he said, "I tell you what, why don't you just pretend you are in my office here and just say what you think you need to say." I replied, "Okay. Why don't you pretend you can see what my middle finger is doing . . . oh wait, you don't believe in nonverbal cues, do you?" Yes. I knew it was a risk, but his stunned silence gave me a chance to remind him how nonverbal behaviors accelerate or undermine progress and this meeting was going to cost a lot in terms of executive time. I suggested that if he wanted to ensure he got a return on his investment, we needed to share the same goals for the day. As a result, we had a much more authentic conversation, made a few mutual agreements, and even built rapport. I not only survived to facilitate difficult conversations about a merger, but this CEO soon began to treat me like his personal counselor. This was not my intent but a good reminder that beneath the bravado, many men crave safe opportunities to be vulnerable. I recommend giving second chances because even if they only work a third of the time, that's still more success than giving up on the first try.

Having a personal chat before a public conversation is a good way to head off many of these games. Asking to hear a few stories about what games group members have regretted in the past frequently earns you a chance to share a few stories yourself. Often the only thing we can agree on first is what we don't want to happen. Granted, there are times when even this subject is irreconcilable. When I am hired to facilitate a work group, I always ask the leader to introduce me with a story that illustrates why they want me there. The nature of the stories they tell is always instructive. Besides, it is a much more collaborative way to start than reading my bio off the website.

The truth is that we can't predict which strategies will work best to de-escalate these territorial games. These ideas are merely a starting place to encourage new conversations and innovative experiments. One thing we can know for sure, is that women need to stop undermining each other and embrace the intersectional goals of protecting life here on earth. When you have a group of sisters who have your back you can feel the power of it. Like this woman who said,

I have a network of women who I rely on and who I trust. At a particular event I came across as sounding kind of tough, so it was important for me to say that I wasn't able

to do what I did without relying on my peer network of other strong women that I trusted. I do that all the time. I mean, it is not always just women, but there's something special about being a woman in a position of power and being able to rely on your "peeps." In a world and an environment that is still really dominated by men, I really do rely on other women.

Not all women will be allies in elevating collaborative narratives to subdue competitive behaviors. But it doesn't hurt to increase the numbers.

CHAPTER SEVEN

CASSANDRA'S PREDICTIONS
Using Power to Protect the Collective

*"If women are not perceived to be fully within
the structures of power, surely it is power that we need to
redefine rather than women."*
—MARY BEARD, *WOMEN AND POWER: A MANIFESTO* (2017)

Many women identify with the Greek myth of Cassandra. On
the surface, this is the story of how the god Apollo granted Cassandra the ability to see the future, then cursed her so no one
would believe her predictions. Most of what we remember about
the myth takes place during the Trojan War. The Greeks pretend
to surrender and offer Troy the victory gift of a huge wooden
horse. Cassandra prophesizes that the gift is a deadly ruse, but
no one believes her. Instead, the Trojans throw open the gates to
accept their victory prize. Greek soldiers hiding inside the gift
horse wait until the Trojans, drunk with booze and glory, fall
asleep, and then they emerge and kill every Trojan man, woman,
and child they find.

The citizens of Troy died because no one believed Cassandra's truthful (but unverifiable) warnings that the Trojan Horse
was not the win it appeared to be. I spent years gathering women's

stories about power before I realized how well this myth embodies the way competitive narratives silence warnings from women (and men) who predict when "winning" endangers collective well-being.

Cassandra represents those of us who anticipate and monitor the way short-term wins might harm collective well-being. Those of us who are concerned about balancing both competitive wins and collective moral wins, such as human rights, climate issues, income equity, and child care, may feel cursedly ignored, but this isn't inevitable. We must learn how to do a better job of telling stories that narrate scenarios from a collective point of view. Then we might convince competitive thinkers to glance up from their tight focus on winning long enough to see a wider-angle view of how an exclusive diet of win/lose reasoning negatively affects the future health of our collective. Many will continue to ignore us, but not all.

We may not want to call ourselves prophets, but how else can we explain the emotional energy that drives us to persist with our warnings? It certainly feels like a curse when our warnings are ignored, discredited, or sidelined. Yet we don't give up. We seem to track collective survival to the point that we feel unsustainable levels of moral distress when we are ignored. Yet this feeling of moral distress could be a beneficial built-in survival warning that triggers bad feelings specifically when behaviors threaten collective survival. It makes sense to think of moral emotions as a kind of survival software for protecting the collective.

Seduced by a Competitive Narrative

The moral of Cassandra's story is not limited to "beware of Greeks bearing gifts." The story also reveals how seductive competitive narratives are and how powerfully they distort perceptions. The Trojans were so blinded by an illusion of victory

DRINKING FROM A DIFFERENT WELL

that they failed to anticipate the collective risk of a suspicious "win." Competitive narratives construct divisive perceptions of the world. Players who interpret life as a game get a thrill out of scoring decisive wins against opponents. Imaginary walls that separate groups into opposing sides make shared goals hard to envision. Meanwhile, those of us who view the world through collaborative narratives anticipate and monitor opportunities to inspire emotions like love, empathy, and sympathy that build relationships and use resources to lift all boats.

Competitive players perceive collaborative goals as competing for limited budgets and time, as well as a distraction from winning. The situation is made worse by the fact that many decisions are now automated to maximize scorecard metrics that allow little room for the story-based reasoning and dialogues that incorporate multiple narratives and are central to collaboration. Little wonder that those of us who attend to both competition and collaboration feel unrepresented and victimized.

The Cassandra story illustrates much about the mortal dangers of interpreting life exclusively through competitive narratives. Consider, for instance, how it warns us about chasing individual wins at the expense of collective well-being. Watching current dangers to health, climate, and environment spiral out of control around us is like watching the Trojans throw open their gates to disaster. The Trojans could only interpret unfolding events through their competitive "Troy First" narrative. They failed to understand Cassandra's warnings, because their maps were too small. They were blind to any warning that might threaten their single-minded pursuit of winning, and that blindness led to their destruction.

Of course, this isn't the only story passed down by our ancestors to document the predictable consequences of competitive greed. King Midas, who got his wish that all he touched would turn to gold, never considered the consequences and ended up killing his daughter, Zoë, when he touched her. In the same way, short-term competitive strategies, such as oil exploitation, can kill future generations through the impacts of climate change. Our ancestors have tried to warn us for eons that pride goeth before a fall. These stories are meant to do more than entertain us: They provide morals of reasoning that can keep us from repeating highly predictable mistakes. Until we back up and find better ways to integrate technologically aided decision-making with the true stories and the moral lessons our ancestors passed down to us, we risk repeating grave mistakes with exponentially larger consequences.

Cassandra and the Golden Apple

The beginning of Cassandra's story reveals a truth that offers us an important lesson for resolving an imbalance between competitive and collaborative narratives. The gods and goddesses want to throw a party to celebrate the wedding of Thetis and Peleus, who eventually became the parents of Achilles, who will become a great warrior and a casualty of the Trojan War. Like any party, this one is shaped by who is invited and by who is not invited.

If you have ever compiled a list of guests, you already know what it's like to wonder if certain people are just too difficult to invite. I imagine many powerful men who dominate boardrooms feel this way about inviting women into the halls of power. When the only goal is winning, inviting women who tell stories of caution or moral obligations ruins the party. Like other myths the Cassandra story does not deny that it is easier, faster, and more efficient in the short term if you don't invite discord. Instead, it concentrates on documenting the long-term price of not inviting discord early when it is more easily resolved.

The all-powerful gods and goddesses planning the wedding

of Thetis and Peleus choose not to invite Eris, the goddess of discord. To be fair, her name describes her personality, and they want their party to be all fun all the time, undisturbed by disagreements. I imagine Eris as an Auntie Mame character who defies conventions and voices uncomfortable truths. Of course, Eris comes to the wedding anyway and, like any good Auntie Mame character, she makes a splash.

According to the myth, the wedding party of gods and goddesses is in full swing when the doors burst open and Eris strides in and tosses out a golden apple inscribed with the words, "For the Fairest." Chaos ensues when the goddesses begin to argue about who is the fairest (don't forget, women indulge in competitive narratives, too). I imagine Eris smiling at the chaos and taking enough time to nod in the direction of those she suspects chose to exclude her.

When everyone looks to Zeus to settle this competition, he sidesteps the difficulty by declaring that Paris, Cassandra's younger brother, will make the decision.

Here's where the myth becomes even more complex, but also more relevant. When Paris was born, Cassandra predicted that he would one day bring about the downfall of Troy. King Priam of Troy, the father of Cassandra and Paris, believed the prediction and ordered the infant to be killed. However, his servant avoided the task by leaving Paris on a mountainside, where shepherds found the infant and raised him. Avoiding difficult decisions is a theme here, though of course I'm not condoning baby killing (this is, after all, a myth). The point is, Cassandra warned of danger and even when she was believed no one followed through on the difficult action that could have avoided the destruction of Troy. As a result, Paris was free to wreak havoc.

So the goddesses Athena, Aphrodite, and Hera descend on Paris as he watches his sheep, and each goddess plies him with

promises and bribes so he will declare her to be the fairest. Hera
offers him power, Athena offers him military might, and Aphrodite, the goddess of love, offers him Helen.

In what may be one of the original #MeToo stories, Helen
was one twin born to Leda, who was seduced by Zeus in the guise
of a swan. The lessons just keep coming: Raping women, seeking
to possess women, none of it turns out well for anyone. Once
Paris decides he wants Helen as his prize, he presents the apple
to Aphrodite, who in turn shifts Helen's love for her husband,
Menelaus, to Paris.

Thus begins the Trojan war, and Cassandra's prediction that
Paris will destroy Troy starts to come true when he sails straight
to Sparta and absconds with Helen. Under the cover of night,
Paris brings Helen with him to Troy, and all hell breaks loose.
The Greek generals Menelaus and Agamemnon (Helen's husband and brother-in-law) gather their armies to extract revenge.
They soon discover that the geography of Troy means the Trojans
are not easily defeated. War, death, and destruction continue for
years. The tit-for-tat killings are too many to list. Among those to
die are Achilles, whose parents' wedding was the scene where this
cascade of tragedy began.

These myths remind us how easy it is to forget when and
how a war began once it gets going. The plots become more
violent and more complicated as fewer characters grasp the big
picture. Humiliations are delivered, and revenge is sought. Once
characters are overcome by desires to win and fears of losing, they
are blinded from imagining, much less pursuing, mutual goals.
This is how avoiding small conflicts leads to bigger conflicts
down the line, and how unchecked competition endangers collective well-being. This myth encapsulates many of the themes of
this book. Let's look at more of them.

Efforts to Discredit Collaborative Narratives

Think about how eager the Trojans were to see their Greek enemies humbled. The joy of winning is often paired with the desire to humiliate opponents. Common metaphors like "crushing the competition" or "destroying rivals" affirm this pattern. But such scorched earth strategies are often harmful, and we burn bridges that we will need in the future. Indeed, few of our metrics track economic losses when "wins" destroy relationships that might have otherwise facilitated beneficial collaboration. These lost opportunities are often dismissed as unverifiable and therefore irrelevant.

Because competitive games require opponents, those of us who reframe enemies as potential collaborators unintentionally ruin the games. It's as if we are suggesting sharing a cup of tea during a knife fight. For many competitive players, collaboration is boring when compared to winning. For a long time, the military used the term "collaborator" to describe traitors who "collaborated with the enemy." Yet there are many times when we could avoid costly consequences with a civil conversation that reconnects opposing sides that have divided a "both/and" paradox into "either/or" reasoning. It is hard to believe in shared goals when adversarial players characterize de-escalation strategies as weak, or, worse, emasculating.

The Mental Load of Predicting Unnecessary Harm

Like Cassandra trying to sound the alarm, women (and men) who anticipate, monitor, and predict the harm competitive reasoning can cause are cursed and excluded. Predictions about the long-term economic threats of climate change, income inequality, and amoral reasoning are mischaracterized as unproven, reactionary, and—the greatest sin—impossible to calculate with accuracy. Sustainability measures that remind us to protect the environment appear to cut into profits and end up cast as a pernicious plot to undermine jobs. Pandemic warnings were discredited as attacks on freedom. The #MeToo movement is often ridiculed. For toxic males, shooting messengers of caution (derogatorily referred to as "social justice warriors") is now a form of entertainment similar to a carnival game, in which what you win matters less than the simple thrill of increasing their scores.

Competitive narratives shrink every paradox (such as sustaining individual as well as collective well-being) into a conflict of interest between factions. Collective stories that promote the benefits of self-restraint end up being characterized as attacks. Competitive narratives funnel all perceptions into maps of "us against them," and those who promote collaborative goals seem to care too much about "them" to be considered "us."

Long ago, the visceral capacity to "sense," predict, and prevent unnecessary harm was called "women's intuition," or "common sense." Today, intuition is often discredited as irrational, as if that renders it useless. This is a flawed criticism when we consider that human behavior is primarily a result of qualitative storied perceptions of belonging that include a multitude of ratios from a multitude of perspectives. Solving global problems depends on our ability to share stories that stretch attention across multiple points of view rather than employing strong-arm tactics to control "the" narrative to a single point of view exclusively derived from ratios so it can be considered "rational."

Recent research into the differences between the way parents share the cognitive burden of raising children seems to illustrate that women spend more time anticipating and monitoring a wider variety of viewpoints than men do. In July 2019, sociology researcher Allison Daminger published in the *American Sociological Review* results that she discovered after interviewers specifically divided the cognitive work of raising a family into four parts: anticipate, identify, decide, and monitor. They discovered that while both men and women participate equally in identifying issues and making decisions, women spend far more time anticipating and monitoring a variety of perspectives. In other words, women do an awful lot of predictive work on behalf of the collective well-being of the family, while men focus their attention on decisions rather than regularly scanning the wider environment to anticipate problems and monitor adverse reactions to those decisions.

For men focused primarily on visible wins, women who invest extra energy to, say, anticipate and arrange doctor visits, monitor recovery, circle back to get lab work, and then facilitate a tough conversation about preventative health care seem to come from left field. Likewise, a female manager who invests extra energy to anticipate and monitor employee satisfaction, arrange social events, monitor personal conflicts, and facilitate reconciliations seems, in effect, to be distracting herself from the scoreboard wins that get her promoted. Yet shutting down our emotional sensors feels too dangerous. If women are indeed saddled with a heightened moral conscience that scans for collective well-being, it isn't hard to see how we don't make ourselves popular by drawing attention to burdens and responsibilities that men neither anticipate nor monitor. If a similar disparity occurs at work, it might also help explain how and why women currently experience more moral distress about workplace issues than men do.

The Blind Spots of Competitive Reasoning
Competitive narratives that only value rational reasoning create strong biases against emotional reasoning. I can't count the times I've seen women who've used emotional reasoning to suggest strategies to avoid hurt feelings being dismissed as ridiculous and

told that anyone offended "will just have to deal with it." A shift in tone might have avoided the problem altogether. The fact that we can't divine a single ratio to predict the costs of hurt feelings or the expense of unchecked greed doesn't mean we should ignore these risks.

Nor is it possible for a single definition of fair to represent the multiple interpretations of what feels fair across multiple viewpoints. Now that we know humans start tracking perceptions of fairness as infants, failing to monitor those perceptions is a critical flaw of competitive narratives. It takes a collaborative point of view to emphasize all of the perceptions that matter when seeking stable long-term global solutions. Ignoring perceptions of fairness and injustice only cost money, time, and efficiency in the long run.

Even though human behavior is not rational, competitive players work on the assumption that everything would work better if it were. Not only is there zero evidence to support this assumption, there is also a zero chance that it will ever happen. The danger of unquestioned faith in scoreboard ratios as the ideal way to make good decisions diminishes our practice of using situational reasoning that takes multiple narratives into account. Yet competitive players continue to promote single rational solutions to correct problems without regard for emotional reasoning. This approach discredits the value of emotional reasoning precisely when we must depend on moral emotions to build alliances, reduce harm, and reverse the erosion of social trust.

Consider the recent pandemic. Statistics that monitor collective well-being have long predicted the likelihood and negative impacts of a viral pandemic. Governments have set up budgets and plans to minimize these collective impacts. Yet in the case of the Covid-19 pandemic, competitive narratives polarized perceptions of risks and undermined faith in a protective perspective by portraying news of the pandemic as a deception. Actions to protect collective well-being were portrayed as attacks on freedom. Predictions of harm were discredited, and efforts to place blame eclipsed efforts to take precautions. The response was politicized as a competitive narrative. People were told that the virus was no worse than a seasonal flu, that it would soon disappear with warm weather, and that it could be cured with bleach or a variety of untested remedies. One faction marshaled racism to blame China instead of instigating collective action to minimize health risks to everyone. A review of the sequence of disinformation illustrates how competitive narratives prize dominance over collective well-being. A central premise of authoritarianism is to maintain dominance at all costs.

When competitive mindsets are fueled by misinformation and blame stories, it is almost impossible to see, much less popularize, collective narratives that pursue collective well-being instead of domination. We can now calculate the losses due to Covid as $29 trillion globally, knowing this staggering figure will not necessarily help us avoid a next time. As long as competitive reasoning reframes the interpretation of collective threats as some sentient enemy's action, we will waste precious time fighting about who is to blame instead of solving our problems.

The Danger of Exclusively Quantitative Risk Management Tools

In order to believe that every win is a good win, one must stifle emotional impulses by categorizing the people who are harmed by those wins as losers. The housing crisis of 2008 was a good example of how "risk management" tools minimized emotional reasoning in order to decrease caution, encourage risks, and increase sales. Encouraging lenders and customers to calculate their risks statistically without inspiring their imaginations to consider the emotional impact of losing a home or dealing with mountains of bad debts made the risk of default feel less risky--as if that were a good thing.

Quantitative formulas for decision-making inhibited the use of interviews and personal stories that might otherwise have reinforced mutual caution between lenders and homeowners. While the industry learned its lesson about loose credit (again), I think we have yet to learn how often competitive narratives undermine harm avoidance. Stories about the development of cryptocurrency give me a feeling of déjà vu all over again. Abstract formulas distract investors from respecting their own internal emotional reasoning. Whether it is a formula to make risk feel less risky or a slogan like HODL to convince investors to "Hold On for Dear Life" to highly risky assets, competitive narratives conspire to distract participants from protecting themselves. This is not to say competitive narratives are always harmful, just that we need collaborative narratives to identify when and how competitive narratives undermine collective goals.

Respecting the Emotional Reasoning of Cognitive Biases

Initially, behavioral economists tried to quantify the emotional forces that make our lives feel meaningful or meaningless. But there were no single ratios that could possibly quantify the range of behavioral responses that result from a tragic loss, burnout, a loving relationship, feeling trustworthy, or the intangible rewards of caregiving. Having failed to quantify emotional reasoning, behavior researchers, including Dan Ariely in his book *Predictably Irrational* (2008), have promoted the view that emotion-informed decisions are irrational errors in judgment.

Researchers have now identified more than 180 cognitive biases (and counting; you might want to Google them) that include "loss aversion," "confirmation bias," and "neglect of probability." Unfortunately, within a competitive point of view, evidence of bias is more likely to be perceived as a weapon rather than a collective resource. The wholesale belief that "irrational" means "wrong" disparages the value of making decisions according to emotional patterns or in response to story-based reasoning. Using technology to "aid" our brains to base all decisions on ratio-based reasoning is analogous to letting autocorrect overrule our text messages.

When competitive frameworks highlight competitive concerns over collaborative well-being, we end up ignoring evolution's solution of using stories to add emotional intelligence to guide decision making. Many survival-related stories remind us to avoid losses once basic needs are met (loss aversion), to seek validating evidence (confirmation bias), or to inspire hope in spite of statistical probabilities (neglect of probability). Without emotional impulses to emphasize belonging, the value of self-discipline, emotional support, and acts of random kindness, we might stop building reserves of social trust.

Flipping the narrative from a competitive point of view to a collaborative one identifies very different ratios that calculate returns on collective well-being and significantly alters the meaning of rational reasoning. That's what happened in the old story of King Solomon, who shifted the narratives of two women locked into competitive claims over an infant by suggesting they each take half. Shifting their narrative to the consequences of a competitive solution immediately highlighted harm to the baby.

Trust Is Irrational within Competitive Narratives

By definition, trust is the faith that someone over whom you have little, or no control will do the "right thing"—act fairly, tell the truth, keep agreements, even when unpredictable circumstances that arise in the future might provide this person with an opportunity to profit by exploiting an unforeseen advantage. By their nature, competitive narratives erode trust by encouraging participants to exploit every situation to their advantage.

Competitive narratives just set us up to look for new and innovative ways to exploit each other. For example, the tracking (basically, surveillance) we experience on social media not only invades our privacy but also erodes trust, in that we can be sure our likes and dislikes are exploited in ways we don't understand. It is no wonder that trust has declined as privacy decreases. Anyone who has felt coerced into signing an impenetrable list of terms and agreements has experienced the impact of competitive reasoning on perceptions of trust. Reasoning based purely on economics deprives us of noticing when emotional decisions such as acts of kindness, empathy, and generosity could have the effect of building and sustaining social trust so it is there when we need it.

Crisis of Trust Due to Misinformation

Pipelines of misinformation designed to lay blame and frame problems as the result of malicious intent by some enemy only reinforce dangerous competitive narratives that pose risks to international peace, endanger the well-being of the planet, and threaten public health. Oversimplifying tough dilemmas with competitive good-guy, bad-guy scenarios fuels mistrust just when we need to expand perspectives and share responsibility to find solutions. Likewise, crafting headlines to nurse racist grudges with false news of paid protestors or cropped images of violence get us no closer to finding shared strategies to mitigate racism. Inventing clickbait headlines like "Pope Francis Shocks World, Endorses Trump for President" profits by inciting emotions of resentment, outrage, and mistrust. Competition for attention has led to an unquestioned norm to believe that "if it bleeds it leads." When stories of conspiracy, lies, and stealing imply that no one is trustworthy, so therefore striving to be trustworthy looks like a weakness. It only takes a dash of emotional reasoning to predict how a constant diet of mistrust will turn out.

Narratives that place blame instead of calling attention to our shared interest in finding solutions distract us from accumulating enough collective power to achieve mutual goals. Without a major effort to reignite global faith that collaborative solutions really do exist and are indeed possible, competitive narratives will continue to inspire silos that hoard resources and propagate divisive perceptions. Humans already have a bad habit of interpreting any crisis as a starting gun to compete to hoard resources (like toilet paper). Priming our imaginations to treat everyone as a competitor produces far more losers than winners.

Failures of Imagination
On September 11, 2001, when the Twin Towers fell in New York City, we shared a profound emotional experience that prompted us to investigate how the attacks happened so that we could avoid ones like them in the future. The experience of that day was so emotional that those of us who witnessed the events still feel the impulse to swap personal stories about where we were when we heard about the planes flying into the World Trade Center and the Pentagon. The subsequent investigation to determine why military intelligence did not predict and prevent these terrorist attacks cited a "failure of the imagination." This term describes any circumstance wherein something seemingly predictable (particularly from hindsight) and exceedingly undesirable is not planned for. The rallying cry of "How did you not know?" applies as well to the pandemic, the Capitol attacks of January 6, 2021, the collapse of the Texas power grid in February 2021, and many more events.

In his book *The Black Swan* (2007), essayist, statistician, and risk analyst Nassim Nicholas Taleb seems to promote this "failure of imagination" theory and claims that most great harms are unexpected because a) "normal" expectations fail to anticipate them, b) the nature of the scientific method and small probabilities render us unable to predict consequential rare events because they are noncomputable, and c) we can blame cognitive biases (aka emotional reasoning) for keeping us blind to uncertainty. Taleb goes on to suggest that our failure to predict catastrophic harm is somehow balanced by an equivalent failure to predict good things, such as major scientific discoveries, historical events, or artistic accomplishments.

Taleb borrows the term "black swan" to describe events that, good or bad, are statistically unpredictable, in the same way that Europeans failed to imagine that there could be black swans until they were discovered in Australia. He suggests that only in hindsight do we wrongly imagine that we might have predicted black swan events.

I disagree. Stories stimulate the imagination to help us predict future possibilities by tracking the emotions and behavioral patterns that apply. If anyone could have visualized a black swan before they saw one, it would have been a storyteller. When we limit ourselves to competitive narratives that can only apply quantifiable analyses, we are the ones who render it impossible to predict these kinds of events. But that isn't the only form of analysis at our disposal. We have collective memories and centuries of stories that specifically predict the negative consequences of greed, the backlash inspired by domination tactics, and the long-term dangers of inequity.

The Power of Storytelling and Emotional Reasoning to Foster Collaboration

Based on *The Black Swan*, I'm guessing that Taleb is not a student of folklore or storytelling. Because in my experience, many of the stories passed down through storytelling traditions do an excellent job stimulating humans both to predict and avoid great harms. The story of David and Goliath warns us against underestimating the power of small groups who believe their cause is just. We have buckets of stories that warn us about what happens when selfish interests override moral concerns, including King Solomon, the Prodigal Son, the Little Match Girl, Narcissus, and Cassandra.

We don't have to be as blind as the Trojans, who chose to chase glory instead of anticipating and monitoring the negative consequences of a dubious win. To foresee future consequences, however, we must understand the value of emotional and story-based reasoning for survival. We must tell our stories and gather more of them to understand better the emotional dynamics we must recruit to protect collective well-being.

However, in order for this to happen, power structures need to start tracking and rewarding collective wins as well as competitive wins. And before that can happen, all of us Cassandras will have to decide to trust our ability to predict future harms even in the face of attack, belittling, or discrediting. We have to stop believing gaslighters who tell us we are wishy-washy just because we are tracking paradoxical goals. We can no longer allow our strength for protecting others to be mislabeled as weakness. We are the ones we have been waiting for.

We can redesign decision procedures to increase the use of collaborative narratives in ways that balance out the shortcomings of competitive narratives. We must market our talent for collaborative thinking to boards who are ready and waiting to resolve paradoxical priorities instead of avoiding them.

We don't know exactly how emotion and imagination work together, but we know they do. Anyone who has walked into a room and without any evidence-based data "just knew" from an internal emotional sensation that there was something wrong knows it works. Sure, this approach is imperfect, but that doesn't mean we should silence these gifts of prediction. We need emotional reasoning to predict the shared consequences of future scenarios in addition to our concern for potential profit margins.

During the 1990s, Texans used quantitative reasoning to calculate that deregulating their power grid would increase speed and efficiency. They were right in the short term. Texas saved money by reducing backup systems and deferring maintenance. But none of the economic projections anticipated the collective negative impact of a winter blizzard in 2021 that produced power outages so severe that a little boy died in his own bed from hypothermia, fuel costs skyrocketed 16,000%, and losses to the community surged to some $90 billion. The danger of ratio-based economic reasoning is how often those who employ it dismiss emotionally motivated reasoning, such as loss aversion, as an error. Meanwhile, our faith in each other and in our institutions relies on emotional reasoning called trust, and trust is not ratio-based.

Melinda French Gates's book, *The Moment of Lift: How Empowering Women Changes the World* (2019), illustrates how important stories really are when it comes to designing workable solutions for global problems. Often these are women's narratives that focus on improving collective well-being, and it is not surprising that women have a lot to say about sourcing collective approaches: We have solid evidence that improving the status of women improves just about every collective measure of health and economic well-being we seek to achieve.

Gathering true stories that track how innovative experiments are adapted to cultural norms often identify solutions that work better than those derived from quantitative analysis. True stories provide vital insights on which emotions best protect us from disease, violence, war, and hoarding. Using stories to guide design incorporates morals that can flip the narrative to focus on avoiding harm, protecting resources, and building trusting relationships as well as scoring wins. Surely this phenomenon should encourage all of us, whether male or female, to pay attention to narratives that focus on improving collective well-being.

My hope is that reading this book provides you with more courage to find and tell the kind of stories that build faith in collective narratives. My hope is that the next time you are criticized as irrational or uninformed you will no longer feel ashamed for leaning into the wisdom of emotional reasoning and personal experiences. Neuroscientists proved long ago that humans literally cannot make decisions without emotions. Now it is time to admit we cannot make reliably good decisions that will protect us from the predictable harm of greed and fear without cultivating collaborative emotions.

So please share your stories. Trust your stories about what power means to you. Split your attention in ways that help you split the attention of those currently mesmerized by competitive reasoning. Build up reserves of stories that prove how "irrational" emotions build faith, reveal otherwise unimagined solutions, and promote mutual benefits that leave plenty of room for profit margins. I hope that you, like Eris the goddess of discord, interrupt exclusive parties to help those who can't yet see what you see to imagine the survival benefits of inviting more women into the halls of power before it is too late.

Niketa's Story

When I first began this research I organized small story-sharing circles with women I admired, whom I invited to my home. One day, surrounded by eight such women, Niketa said "I don't have a story about being powerful, but I do have a story about feeling powerless that I want to share." I am embarrassed to admit it, but I put my pen and paper down thinking "That's not why we are here, but I will listen." I wish I had taken notes. The good news is that I kept Niketa's phone number. I'm thrilled to share her story in the context of where she is now. She has traveled from powerless to powerful.

Niketa's original story about feeling powerless occurred in 2016 in South Sudan, after she had attended medical school and before she found a residency.

"They had signed a peace agreement to end the civil war, so I accepted a job as a program manager doing research in Juba, South Sudan. I remember asking about the specifics of our emergency evacuation plan, and while I was assured there was one, no one shared the specifics. Every time I asked, I was treated like a troublemaker. God, I wish I'd pressed the point anyway. Not long after I arrived, fighting erupted again between government and opposition soldiers. One of my researchers in the field was jailed and tortured. We got him out but only through bribes. A lot of our work required bribes at that time.

Soldiers on both sides weren't being paid. They were angry and itching for revenge. I lived in an apartment in a tall building, and while it was illegal to film in South Sudan, some jackass got up on the roof of my building with a camera. That gave the soldiers all the permission they needed to start shooting and entering our building to

*search for him. We stayed away from the windows. I joined
my neighbor. We hid in her bathroom listening to the
gunshots and the soldiers banging on every door. We were
terrified. Two more women joined us. One was so hysterical I feared she would attract the soldiers. A call to my
boss, who was safe in Kenya, proved that in spite of all her
assertions about an evacuation plan, there wasn't one. I've
never been so afraid in my life. I had a satellite phone, and
I knew that if it was found it would make things worse for
me. At some point my neighbor said, 'I will answer if they
knock so you three can stay safe here.' She really was ready
to make that sacrifice.*

*Then the power went off. That's a strategy they use to
reduce the fighting. But then we heard mortars dropping.
We lay close to the ground and kept texting anyone who
might help. At another location soldiers killed a guard
and began combing the rooms for women to rape. They
found them. The soldiers used rape as a war tactic as well
as a way to celebrate victories. I have never felt so powerless
in my life.*

*As a child I could negotiate just about any situation.
The teachers said only boys could help stack chairs after
school, but I showed them I could stack chairs, too. When
I went to the library and was told one section was too difficult for me, I read out loud for the librarian and was given
access. But I couldn't negotiate my way out of the lies I was
told and the war that raged around me. I was powerless."*

After sharing her story Niketa wasn't the only one with tears in
her eyes. It was a reality check to remember how powerless wom-
en feel when threats of rape or death strip us of alternatives. Today I'm glad to report that Niketa is anything but powerless. She

is currently enrolled as the chief resident at a prestigious medical school studying the collective goal of preventative medicine. She worked in an ER in Detroit during the worst of Covid and then spent time in the Navajo nation. She is beautiful, smart, and strong, and one day I expect she will use her power to inform the entire field of preventative medicine. It's not irrelevant that she is also Black. White women have so much to learn from Black women, and it's time we realized that. Black women have centuries of experience protecting those they love from oppressive systems. One of the main reasons women are demanding more power is that while we want to thrive as much as the guys do, we also want to protect the people we love and the people who most deserve protection from unchecked competitive narratives and oppressive systems. We persevere. We are still speaking. And we won't stop until we are heard.

If you would like to share your story,
read more stories, and swap ideas on how
to reframe what power means in action,
visit: **Differentwell.com**

ACKNOWLEDGMENTS

Thank you to the many generous storytellers who trained me
to respect the habits and intentions of traditional forms of
storytelling: Judith Black, Milbre Burch, Nancy Donoval,
Elizabeth Ellis, Heather Forest, Doug Lipman, Angela Lloyd,
Michael D. McCarty, Loren Niemi, Laura Packer, Laura Simms,
Joseph Sobol, Ed Stivender and National Storytelling Network.

And thank you Stephen Brewer, editor extraordinaire, for all
your patience and generous support.

To Laura Guyer, who not only believed in this project but
helped me recruit women to interview. Laura you renewed my
motivation. I can't imagine finishing this book without your
support. Thank you.

To all my girlfriends over the years who have helped me figure
out what power means in action! Thank you to Mary Alice
Arthur, Bonnie Bayer, Nettie Brown, Jo Linn Whitsell Burt,

Michele Kim Carter, Steffi Chaffee, Robin Clawson,
Kathy Cole, Christina Colombo, Jennifer Courtney,
ML Dumars, Cheryl DeCiantis, Brandy and Sherry Decker,
Karen Dietz, Wendy Hamilton-Hoelscher, Jennifer Hill,
Debbie Hollis, Frances Kelley, Valerie Loridans, Cassie
McDaniels, Pam Woodhall McGrath, Julie Mundy-Taylor,
Ruth Wong Nalley, Wesley Hall Parker, Thaler Pekar,
Debra Robertson, Terri Roeder, Kay Kellogg Raharjo, Jere Saur,
Tilottama Shome, Eva Snijders, Syble Solomon, SB Rawz,
Lea Ann Wade, Nikita Williams, and every woman who shared
her stories with me.

And to my dear departed friends Meena Wilson and
Elizabeth Carlson I miss you.

But most of all I want to thank Christopher Jones whose unfail-
ing encouragement, support, love and understanding helped me
finish this project. Chris, I couldn't have done it without you.

BIBLIOGRAPHY

Achiron, Reuwen, Shlomo Lipitz, and Anat Achiron. "Sex-Related Differences in the Development of the Human Fetal Corpus Callosum: *In Utero* Ultrasonographic Study." *Prenatal Diagnosis* 21, no. 2 (2001): 116-120.

Albright, Madeleine. *Madam Secretary: A Memoir.* New York: Miramax Books, 2003.

Allen, L. S., and R. A. Gorski. "Sexual Dimorphism of the Anterior Commissure and Massa Intermedia of the Human Brain." *Journal of Comparative Neurology* 31, no. 1 (1991): 97-104. doi:10.1002/cne.903120108

Angier, Natalie. *Woman: An Intimate Geography.* New York: Houghton Mifflin Harcourt, 1999; reprint, Anchor Books, 2000.

Auyeung, Bonnie, Simon Baron-Cohen, Emma Ashwin, Rebecca Knickmeyer, Kevin Taylor, Gerald Hackett, and Melissa Hines. "Fetal Testosterone Predicts Sexually Differentiated Childhood Behavior in Girls and in Boys." *Psychological Science* 20, no. 2 (2009): 144-148. doi:10.1111 /j.1467-9280.2009.02279.x

Berenbaum, Sheri A., and Elizabeth Snyder. "Early Hormonal Influences on Childhood Sex-Typed Activity and Playmate Preferences: Implications for the Development of Sexual Orientation." *Developmental Psychology* 31, no. 1 (1995): 31-42. https://doi.org/10.1037/0012-1649.31.1.31

Bolla, K. I., D. A. Eldreth, J. A. Matochik, and Cadet, J. L. "Sex-Related Differences in a Gambling Task and Its Neurological Correlates." *Cerebral Cortex* 14, no. 11 (2004): 1226-1232. doi:10.1093/cercor/bhh083

Brough, Aaron R., James E. B. Wilkie, Jingjing Ma, Mathew S. Isaac, and David Gal. "Is Eco-Friendly Unmanly? The Green-Feminine Stereotype and Its Effect on Sustainable Consumption." *Journal of Consumer Research* 43, no. 4 (2016): 567-82. https://doi.org/10.1093/jcr/ucw044

Brown, Brené. *I Thought It Was Just Me (But It Isn't): Women Reclaiming Power and Courage in a Culture of Shame,* New York: Gotham Books, 2007.

Brown, Brené. *Rising Strong: The Reckoning, the Rumble, the Revolution.* New York: Random House, 2015.

Bryce, Robert. *Pipe Dreams: Greed, Ego, and the Death of Enron.* New York: PublicAffairs, 2002.

Cahill, L., R. J. Haier, N. S. White, J. Fallon, J. Kilpatrick, C. Lawrence, S. G. Potkin, and M. T. Alkire. "Sex-Related Difference in Amygdala Activity during Emotionally Influenced Memory Storage." *Neurobiology of Learning and Memory* 75, no. 1 (2001): 1-9. doi:10.1006/nlme.2000.3999

Close, Henry T. *Metaphor in Psychotherapy: Clinical Applications of Stories and Allegories.* San Luis Obispo, CA: Impact Publishers, 1998.

Clinton, Hillary Rodham. *Living History.* New York: Simon & Schuster, 2003.

Damasio, Antonio. *The Feeling of What Happens: Body and Emotion in the Making of Consciousness.* New York: Harcourt, 1999.

De Bono, Edward. *I Am Right, You Are Wrong.* New York: Viking Press, 1991.

De Courten-Myers, Gabrielle M., Theodore Rabinowicz, Jean MacDonald-Comber Petetot, Peter S. Gartside, David Sheyn, and Tony Sheyn. "Structure of the Cerebral Cortex in Men and Women." *Journal of Neuropathology and Experimental Neurology* 61, no. 1 (2002): 46-57. https://doi.org/10.1093/jnen/61.1.46

Dewing, Phoebe, Tao Shi, Steve Horvath, and Eric Vilain. "Sexually Dimorphic Gene Expression in Mouse Brain Precedes Gonadal Differentiation." *Molecular Brain Research* 118, nos. 1-2 (2003): 82-90. doi:10.1016/S0169-328X(03)00339-5

Diversity Best Practices Staff. *WOW! Facts,* 13th Edition. Washington, DC: Business Women's Network and Diversity Best Practices, 2015.

Dolcos, Florin, Yuta Katsumi, Chen Shen, Paul C. Bogdan, Suhnyoung Jun, Ryan Larsen, Wendy Heller, Kelly Freeman Bost, and Sanda Dolcos. "The Impact of Focused Attention on Emotional Experience: A Functional MRI Investigation." *Cognitive, Affective, & Behavioral Neuroscience* 20, no. 5 (2020): 1011-1026. doi:10.3758/s13415-020-00816-2

Doyle, Glennon. *Untamed.* New York: Dial Press, 2020.

Ensler, Eve. *The Vagina Monologues.* New York: Villard, 1998.

Evans, Gail. *Play Like a Man, Win Like a Woman: What Men Know about Success That Women Need to Learn.* New York: Broadway Books, 2000.

Forbes, Geraldine. *Women in Modern India* (South Asian edition). Delhi: Cambridge University Press, 2000.

Frederikse, Melissa, Angela Lu, Elizabeth Aylward, Patrick Barta, and Godfrey Pearlson. "Sex Differences in the Inferior Parietal Lobule." *Cerebral Cortex* 9, no. 8 (1999): 896-901. doi.org/10.1093/cercor/9.8.896

Fromm, Erich. *Escape from Freedom.* New York: Rinehart & Company, 1941; reprints, 1969, 1994.

Funk, Jeanne B. "Reevaluating the Impact of Video Games." *Clinical Pediatrics* 32, no. 2 (1993): 86-90. doi.10.1177/000992289303200205

Garrels, Anne. *Naked in Baghdad: The Iraq War as Seen by NPR's Correspondent Anne Garrels.* New York: Farrar, Straus & Giroux, 2003.

Gilligan, Carol. *In a Different Voice: Psychological Theory and Women's Development.* Cambridge, MA: Harvard University Press, 1982; reprints, 1993, 2001.

Gilligan, Carol. *The Birth of Pleasure.* New York: Alfred A. Knopf, 2002.

Gladwell, Malcolm. *The Tipping Point: How Little Things Can Make a Big Difference.* Boston: Little, Brown and Company, 2000.

Goleman, Daniel. *Emotional Intelligence: Why It Can Matter More than IQ.* New York: Bantam Books, 1995.

Goldberg, Elkhonon. *The Executive Brain: Frontal Lobes and the Civilized Mind.* New York: Oxford University Press, 2001.

Goldstein, Jill M., Larry J. Seidman, Nicholas J. Horton, Nikos Makris, David N. Kennedy, Verne S. Caviness, Jr., Stephen V. Faraone, and Ming T. Tsuang. "Normal Sexual Dimorphism of the Adult Human Brain Assessed by In Vivo Magnetic Resonance Imaging." *Cerebral Cortex* 11, no. 6 (2001): 490-497. doi.10.1093/cercor/11.6.490

Good, C. D., I. Johnsrude, J. Ashburner, R. N. Henson, K. J. Friston, and R. S. Frackowiak. "Cerebral Asymmetry and the Effects of Sex and Handedness on Brain Structure: A Voxel-Based Morphometric Analysis of 465 Norman Adult Human Brains." *Neuroimage* 14, no. 3 (2001): 685-700. doi:10.1006/nimg.2001.0857

Graham, Katharine. *Personal History.* New York: Vintage Books, 1997.

Grön, Georg, Arthur Wunderlich, Manfred Spitzer, Reinhard Tomczak, and Matthias Riepe. "Brain Activation during Human Navigation: Gender-Different Neural Networks as Substrate of Performance." *Nature Neuroscience* 3, no. 4 (2000): 404-408. doi:10.1038/73980

Gur, Ruben C., Faith Gunning-Dixon, Warren B. Bilker, and Raquel E. Gur. "Sex Differences in Temporo-Limbic and Front Brain Volumes of Healthy Adults." *Cerebral Cortex* 12, no. 9 (2002): 998-1003. doi:10.1093/cercor/12.9.998

Gur, Ruben C., Bruce I. Turetsky, Mie Matsui, Michelle Yan, Warren Bilker, Paul Hughett, and Raquel E. Gur. "Sex Differences in Brain Gray and White Matter in Healthy Young Adults: Correlations with Cognitive Performance." *Journal of Neuroscience* 19, no. 10 (1999): 4065-4072. doi:10.1523/JNEUROSCI.19-10-04065.1999

Heffernan, Margaret. 2002. "The Female CEO." In *Fast Company Magazine,* August 2002, 61:58.

Hill, Alex K., Drew H. Bailey, and David A. Puts. "Gorillas in Our Midst? Human Sexual Dimorphism and Contest Competition in Men." Chapter 15 in Michel Tibayrenc and

Francisco J. Ayala, eds., *On Human Nature: Biology, Psychology, Ethics, Politics, and Religion*. Cambridge, MA: Academic Press, 2016. https://doi.org/10.1016/B978-0-12-420190-3.00015-6

Katherine, Anne. *Where to Draw the Line: How to Set Healthy Boundaries Every Day*. New York: Fireside, 2000.

Killgore, William D., Mika Oki, and Deborah A. Yurgelun-Todd. "Sex-Specific Developmental Changes in Amygdala Responses to Affective Faces." *NeuroReport* 12, no. 2 (2001): 427-433. doi:10.1097/00001756-200102120-00047

Kline, John P., Ginette C. Blackhart, and Gary E. R. Schwartz. "Gender Specificity of Resting Anterior Electroencephalographic Asymmetry and Defensiveness in the Elderly." *The Journal of Gender-Specific Medicine* 2, no. 4 (1999): 35-39.

Lakoff, George, and Mark Johnson. *Philosophy in the Flesh: The Embodied Mind and Its Challenge to Western Thought*. New York: Basic Books, 1999.

Larsen, Clark Spencer. "Equality for the Sexes in Human Evolution? Early Hominid Sexual Dimorphism and Implications for Mating Systems and Social Behavior." *Proceedings of the National Academy of Sciences of the United States of America* 100, no. 16 (2003): 9103-9104. https://doi.org/10.1073/pnas.1633678100

Latifah, Queen. *Ladies First: Revelations of a Strong Woman*. New York: Quill, 2000.

LeDoux, Joseph. *The Emotional Brain: The Mysterious Underpinnings of Emotional Life*. New York: Simon & Schuster, 1996.

Lesser, Elizabeth. *Cassandra Speaks: When Women Are the Storytellers, the Human Story Changes*. New York: Harper Wave, 2020.

Maggio, Rosalie. *The New Beacon Book of Quotations by Women*. Boston: Beacon Press, 1996.

Mitchell, Tejal N., Samantha L. Free, Martin Merschhemke, Louis Lemieux, Sanjay M. Sisodiya, and Simon D. Shorvon. "Reliable Callosal Measurement: Population Normative Data Confirm Sex-Related Differences." *American Journal of Neuroradiology* 24, no. 3 (2003): 410-418.

Moir, Anne, and Bill Moir, *Why Don't Men Iron: The Fascinating and Unalterable Differences between Men and Women*. New York: Citadel Press, 1999.

Muoio, Anna. *Women and Men, Work and Power*. In *Fast Company Magazine,* January 1998, 13:71.

Niemi, Loren, and Elizabeth Ellis. *Inviting the Wolf In: Thinking about Difficult Stories*. Little Rock, Ark.: August House Publishers, 2001.

Noor, Queen. *Leap of Faith: Memoirs of an Unexpected Life*. New York: Miramax Books, 2003.

Ornstein, Robert. *The Right Mind: Making Sense of the Hemispheres*. New York: Harcourt Brace, 1997.

Pease, Allen, and Barbara Pease. *Why Men Don't Listen and Women's Can't Read Maps*. London: Orion Publishing, 1998.

Pearson, Allison. *I Don't Know How She Does It: The Life of Kate Reddy, Working Mother*. New York: Alfred A. Knopf, 2002.

Person, Ethel S. *Feeling Strong: The Achievement of Authentic Power*. New York: William Morrow and Company, 2002.

Pert, Candace B. *Molecules of Emotion: Why You Feel the Way You Feel*. New York: Scribner, 1997.

Phillips, Micheal D., Mark J. Lowe, Joseph T. Lurito, Mario Dzemidzic, Yang Wang, and Vincent P. Mathews. "Temporal Lobe Activation Demonstrates Sex-Based Differences during Passive Listening." *Radiology* 220, no. 1 (2001): 202-207. doi:10.1148/radiology.220.1.r01jl34202

Popcorn, Faith, and Lys Marigold. *Eve-olution: Understanding Women – Eight Essential Truths That Work in Your Business and Your Life*. New York: Hyperion, 2001.

Sandstrom, N. J., J. Kaufman, and S. A. Huettel. "Males and Females Use Different Distal Cues in a Virtual Environment Navigation Task." *Brain Research: Cognitive Brain Research* 6, no. 4 (1998): 351-360.

Schneider, Frank, Ute Habel, Christoph Kessler, Jasmin B. Salloum, and Stefan Posse. "Gender Differences in Regional Cerebral Activity during Sadness." *Human Brain Mapping* 9, no. 4 (2000): 226-238. doi:10.1002/(sucu)1097-0193(200004)9

Schutzgruber, Barbara. *Beyond the Sword Maiden*. Marion, MI: Parkhurst Brothers Publishers, 2018.

Seligman, Martin E. P. *What You Can Change and What You Can't: Learning to Accept Who You Are*. New York: Fawcett Columbine, 1993.

Shaywitz, Bennett A., Sally E. Shaywitz, et al. "Sex Differences in the Functional Organization of the Brain for Language." *Nature* 373, no. 6515 (1995): 607-609.

Shors, Tracey J. and George Miesegaes. "Testosterone *in Utero* and at Birth Dictates How Stressful Experiences Will Affect Learning in Adulthood." *Proceedings of the National Academy of Sciences of the United States of America* 99, no. 21 (2002): 13955-13960. https://doi.org/10.1073/pnas.202199999

Simmons, Annette. *The Story Factor*, 3d edition. New York: Basic Books, 2019.

Simmons, Annette. *Whoever Tells the Best Story Wins*. New York: HarperCollins, 2007.

Sobol, Joseph. *Liars, Damn Liars, and Storytellers: Essays on Traditional and Contemporary Storytelling*. Knoxville, TN: University of Tennessee Press, 2020.

Tannen, Deborah. *Talking from 9 to 5: How Women's and Men's Conversational Styles Affect Who Gets Heard, Who Gets Credit, and What Gets Done at Work*. New York: William Morrow and Company, 1994.

Tannen, Deborah. *The Argument Culture: Moving from Debate to Dialogue.* New York: Random House, 1998.

Taylor, Shelley E. *The Tending Instinct: How Nurturing Is Essential for Who We Are and How We Live.* New York: Times Books, 2002.

Tenneson, Joyce. *Wise Women: A Celebration of Their Insights, Courage, and Beauty.* Boston: Little, Brown and Company, 2002.

Terlecki, Melissa S., Jennifer Brown, Lindsey Harner-Steciw, John Irvin-Hannum, Nora Marchetto-Ryan, Linda Ruhl, and Jennifer Wiggins. "Sex Differences and Similarities in Video Game Experience, Preferences, and Self-Efficacy: Implications for the Gaming Industry." *Current Psychology* 30, no. 1 (2011): 22-33. https://doi.org/10.1007/s12144-010-9095-5

Toffler, Barbara. *Final Accounting: Ambition, Greed, and the Fall of Arthur Andersen.* New York: Broadway Books, 2003.

Wager, Tor D., K. Luan Phan, Israel Liberzon, and Stephan F. Taylor. "Valence, Gender, and Lateralization of Functional Brain Anatomy in Emotion: A Meta-Analysis of Findings from Neuroimaging." *Neuroimage* 19, no. 3 (2003): 513-531. doi:1-.1016/s1053-8119(03)00078-8

Wilhelm, Claudia. "Gender Role Orientation and Gaming Behavior Revisited: Examining Mediated and Moderated Effects." *Information, Communication & Society* 21, no. 2 (2018): 224-240. doi:10.1080/1369118X.2016.1271902

Wiseman, Rosalind. *Queen Bees and Wannabes: Helping Your Daughter Survive Cliques, Gossip, Boyfriends, and Other Realities of Adolescence.* New York: Three Rivers Press, 2003.

Wood, Gwendolyn, and Tracey J. Shors. "Stress Facilitates Classical Conditioning in Males, but Impairs Classical Conditioning in Females through Activational Effects of Ovarian Hormones." *Proceedings of the National Academy of Sciences of the United States of America* 95, no. 7 (1998): 4066-4071. doi:10.1073/pnas.95.7.4066

Zichy, Shoya, *Women and the Leadership Q: The Breakthrough System for Achieving Power and Influence.* New York: McGraw-Hill, 2001.

INDEX

war narratives, 72–74
Mori, Yoshiro, 93
Mycorrhiza (journal), 66

narratives, 12–13
negative feminine traits, 58–59
New York Times (newspaper), 52, 66
Niketa's story, 137–39
9/11, 132
Norway, 92

The 100 Best Business Books of All Time, 7
One Thousand and One Nights, 53–54
overtalking, 106–7

Parker, Wesley Hall, 56–57
performance, 70–71
performance-based frame, 45–46
perseveration, 87
points of view, 10–11, 38–40, 81, 125
Portugal, 92
power
 ambiguity, 102
 bad power, 17, 26, 51, 62–63, 108–9
 caregiving/caretaking, 60–61
 collective well-being, 119
 competition and cooperation, 43–48
 definitions of, 61–63
 emotional rewards, 43
 empathy, 52
 female leadership, 88–90
 gender differences, 10, 16–18, 66–67, 69–70, 75–79, 90
 good power, 17, 26, 51, 62–63, 69
 helping, 33–34

home and work, 28–29
 internal conflicts, 100–101
 internal feedback, 42–43
 internal guidance systems, 81–82
 loss avoidance, 81
 outside of financial gain, 26
 power-in-action, 3–5
 protection, 22–23
 traditional ideas about, 26–29, 36–37
 trust, 20–21
 war narratives, 73
 women's power preferences, 77–79
powerlessness, 137–39
The Power of Vulnerability (Brown), 34–35
power-over, 26, 29, 36, 88, 90
power-with, 26, 29–30, 36, 90
Predictably Irrational (Ariely), 129
preferences, 42, 70, 75–76
privacy, 68, 131
protection, 22–23, 47–48, 80, 82, 88–90, 101, 116–17, 119, 128
PTSD, 106

quantitative reasoning, 135–36
quantitative risk management tools, 128–29

ratio-based reasoning, 80, 95, 130, 135
rational reasoning, 126, 130
ratio-to-kill, 72
reciprocal generosity, 27–28
reciprocity, 68
relational aspects of implementation, 38–40
resistance, 22
responsiveness, 76
reward systems, 80–81
risk aversion, 46

READING GUIDE

Simmons says, "I find that true stories about real life often reveal truths that run deeper than traditional theories and dictionary definitions."

PERSONAL SELF EVALUATION

Before you jump into the book, take a minute to tune into your own personal interpretations about what power means in action.

1. Do you consider yourself powerful? Rate yourself on a scale of 1 to 10. What memories come up as you try to come up with a number? Who do you compare yourself to? What does this tell you about what power means to you?
2. What emotional reactions do you have when you hear the word "power"?
3. Create your own list of the advantages and disadvantages of having power.
4. Who had power in your family? What were the lessons (spoken and unspoken)?
5. Were you taught to expect to have power?
6. What's your current comfort level with taking a position that is considered powerful?

I'd love to hear your answers to these questions. Please send an email to annette@differentwell.com or post a comment on the blog on differentwell.com. Your contribution helps expand the conversation so we can learn more about how to change what power means in action.

BOOK GROUP
DISCUSSION GUIDE

INTRODUCTION

"We asked our network of clients and friends to "name a powerful woman who might be willing to share a story." After we interviewed the women they nominated, we asked those powerful women to nominate other powerful women."

Without thinking too much about it, list three women you know personally who you consider to be powerful. What do these women have in common? What differences might you notice if you were to compare them to a similar list of powerful men?

The question *"On a scale of one to ten, how powerful are you?"* was used to anchor interviewees firmly in their personal experiences of power rather than the theories we've been taught to believe. Go around the room and share the number you might give yourself and talk about how you chose that number.

What public leaders today do you consider to be moral? immoral? Name the actions and behaviors that justify your opinions. What does morality have to do with power?

Do you think gender is a factor of nature or nurture? Or, do you agree with Simmons, who seems to believe that these discussions distract us from finding solutions?

CHAPTER ONE
MY OWN STORY

Have you ever had an experience like the one Simmons describes at the beginning of Chapter One? If so, what were you trying to achieve? How did your goals threaten a man's power? What was he trying to achieve?

Simmons says her *"strategy was to pretend the incident with Ian didn't matter."* What are the advantages and disadvantages when we ignore these kinds of incidents?

Who was the most powerful person you knew during your childhood? What did you learn about power from that person? Have you re-evaluated some of the lessons you learned?

Why do you think Simmons started the book with her own story? Do you think power is a subjective or an objective topic?

CHAPTER TWO
STORIES WOMEN TELL ABOUT POWER THAT MEN DON'T

Come up with your own story about a time when you used your power in action and share it with the group. In the story, did you pursue goals of dominance/control? participation/collaboration? or both?

Which of the three stories presented in Chapter Two is your favorite? Why?

Simmons creates a list of the tactics she found to be more prevalent in women's stories of power than in men's stories of power. Have you had your own experiences when using your power required you to recruit one or more of these tactics? Which of these created the biggest challenges for you?

Trust in your ability to reason
Resist gaslighting
Stick to your own narrative
Prioritize a moral win
Construct a shared frame of reference
Define power outside of financial gain
Use internal reasoning to justify unpaid labor
Build social trust by showing faith in others
Merge the contexts of home and work
Consider power-with versus power-over
Choosing to help
Becoming vulnerable in order to learn
The influence of moral emotions
Break rules

CHAPTER THREE
SEXUAL DIMORPHISM
The Evolution of Male and Female Points of View

Simmons writes, "From an evolutionary point of view, it makes sense that men and women might have naturally evolved two complementary points of view that highlight slightly different aspects of the implementation of change." Can you see any benefit for nature/nurture to allocate different concerns according to gender?

Hummingbirds illustrate the concept of sexual dimorphism. What other species can you think of that benefit from developing different but complementary habits and desires? Do you see similar differences among humans?

Do you think you approach situations from a stance of Competition or Collaboration?

"Francesca Gino, Caroline Ashley Wilmuth, and Alison Wood Brooks conducted a total of nine studies published by Harvard in 2015 that indicate that even when women believe they could win a top position if they wanted to, they often chose instead to avoid the negative outcomes they anticipated as a result of "winning." Have you ever avoided a job to avoid negative consequences? What turned you off? What tradeoffs were you not willing to make?

Simmons says, *"Women may tend to draw circles of moral concern that include people and issues that men interpret as being outside their circle of concern."* What people are currently being ignored from decision making that concerns the environment, climate, poverty, and other issues relating to collective wellbeing? In specific, can you think of issues of crucial importance to women that are being made by groups that exclude women?

It's a given that many people are excluded from decisions that affect the welfare of us all. How do you think this will impact the wellbeing of the human species?

Moral emotions seem essential to the survival of our species. In the book *Just Babies: The Origins of Good and Evil* (2013), about the genetic origins of morality, Yale psychology professor Paul Bloom confirms: "There are hard-wired moral universals."

Simmons cites examples of three-month old babies who favor those characters who help over those who hinder. What moral tendencies have you noticed in children? Do adults display the same moral tendencies? If not, why do you think that is?

Do you notice a difference between the movies and games that men and women enjoy? How would it help our collective survival if men enjoyed the same pastimes that women do?

CHAPTER FOUR
FEMALE VERSUS MALE CONCEPTS OF POWER

"For some women the power to achieve a moral "win" eclipses the value of more tangible economic wins."

Consider the stories you shared earlier to define what power means to you. Were your goals in your story about power easy to measure in quantitative terms (that is, more money or a promotion). If not, how did you know you had achieved your goals.

How do you distinguish "good" power from "bad" power?

Is there an advantage in claiming that power is neither good nor bad?

Simmons mentions the *"vast underground network of roots and fungi called mycorrhizae. These deliver chemical, hormonal, and slow-pulsing electrical messages to 'mother trees' that respond by redistributing water, nutrients, and even airspace to protect entire forests. The unseen messages of the mycorrhizal system identify stockpiled resources, redistribute extra resources to the needy, warn of danger, support slow growth, and waste nothing."* Do you think the human systems that currently allocate water, nutrients and airspace are similarly collaborative?

Who benefits if concerns for the environment or mask wearing are labeled as feminine, weak, or "girlie"? What is the impact of labeling these kinds of concerns as "negatively" feminine? What would need to change for these kinds of concerns to be considered "positively" feminine?

What aspects of technology facilitate this idea of "negatively" feminine? Do you see male biases at work in technology that limit your ability to pursue moral goals?

Simmons mentions the *combat historian S. L. A. Marshall estimated that only 20% of World War II soldiers actually pulled the trigger in fighting situations [so] the military developed new training to automate behavior and desensitize soldiers to their emotions in ways that increased the ratio-to-kill up to 85% during the Vietnam War. The ratio-to-kill continues to "improve."* What "improvements" have you witnessed personally that didn't seem like improvements to you? Did you speak up? What were the consequences for speaking up?

Have you been in situations where you could use your power to achieve goals that seem inefficient from a male perspective? For instance, using work time to organize pro bono activities?

CHAPTER FIVE

HOW WOMEN'S NARRATIVES CHANGE THE STORY

Simmons presents two lists of the plots of men's and women's stories about power on pages 77 and 78. Did you have an immediate sense of which list seemed more female? What stood out as distinctively female or male?

Have you been in a situation where your goals were characterized as "irrational" or "ridiculous?"

Remember the story about Simmons asking Goldratt to re-think his interpretation of the results of his cognitive bias test? In your own decision making do you think you acknowledge emotional reasoning as well as quantitative reasoning?

Were there any major decisions where you trusted your intuition more than numbers and charts? Share this story with the group.

CHAPTER SIX
WHAT TO DO WHEN COMPETITIVE GAMES THREATEN COLLABORATIVE PREFERENCES

In the story Simmons tells about using poetry to shift the norms of a work group away from a perspective of competition towards a perspective of collaboration. What might be the benefit of making these points of view visible to the whole group before their budget meeting? Would this be as effective as leading up to these points of views with the poem? What emotions are vital to adopting a perspective of collaboration? What emotions become troublesome?

Simmons list ten games that competitive players use to undermine collaborative efforts that appear to threaten their goals. Have you encountered any of the territorial games mentioned in this chapter?

The Ten Territorial Games

Occupation | Strategic Non-Compliance
Intimidation | Information Manipulation
Filibuster | Shunning
Camouflage | Powerful Alliances
Invisible Walls | Discrediting

Which games do you play? What do you think of Simmons' advice for responding to these games?

CHAPTER SEVEN
CASSANDRA'S PREDICTIONS: USING POWER
TO PROTECT THE COLLECTIVE

What can we glean from the story about Cassandra about how competitive perspectives blind us from anticipating and avoiding predictable harm?

Why does Simmons bring up the character of Eris, the Goddess of Discord, and how does this character relate to the circumstances we face today?

What is the danger of expecting quantitative models to predict the future for us? How can business processes better integrate qualitative and emotional reasoning into the mix now that many decisions have been automated to use metrics instead of emotions? How can we encourage businesses to keep taking risks at the same time they do a better job of preventing harm to people and places?

Can you think of a time when strong emotional impulses caused you to make an "irrational" decision that turned out to be a good decision? What would have happened if you tried to make a decision that was strictly rational?

How do competitive narratives justify the use of misinformation?

The purpose of this book was to take you on a self-awareness journey to see if you have been censoring yourself to fit into a definition of power that doesn't feel powerful. Did you find cause to re-consider what power means to you? Do you plan to make any changes as a result?

Annette Simmons has travelled internationally
while working with government, business, religious, and
educational organizations. Her ability to deliver practical,
easily implemented solutions when groups were antagonistic
or deadlocked has gained her an international
reputation in group dynamics.

" I CAN DO NO HARM", YOU INEVITAB...
will told y...
have to o...
the minim...
RISK A SOM...
as posi...

(My FUTURE
1ST PHD
GRADUATE)!
DEAR DR. ~~~~~~~~~~~~~~

↑

DEAR DRA. LYSANDRA
PEREZ ¿? S

↑

MENTORED BY:
DEAR DRA. CRISTINA ALFARO

↑

MENTORED BY:
DEAR DRA. ANTONIA DARDER

↑
MENTORED BY:
DEAR DR. PAOLO FREIRE

Lysandra Perez (signature)

PM. (signature)

DRA. PEREZ

DRA. LYSANDRA
PEREZ

DRA. PEREZ